DVD Confidential

Hundreds of Hidden Easter Eggs Revealed!

 OSBORNE

DVD Confidential

Hundreds of Hidden Easter Eggs Revealed!

Marc Saltzman

Osborne

New York • Chicago • San Francisco
Lisbon • London • Madrid • Mexico City • Milan
New Delhi • San Juan • Seoul • Singapore • Sydney • Toronto

The McGraw·Hill Companies

McGraw-Hill/Osborne
2600 Tenth Street
Berkeley, California 94710
U.S.A.

To arrange bulk purchase discounts for sales promotions, premiums, or fund-raisers, please contact McGraw-Hill/Osborne at the above address. For information on translations or book distributors outside the U.S.A., please see the International Contact Information page at the end of this book.

DVD Confidential: Hundreds of Hidden Easter Eggs Revealed!

1234567890 DOC DOC 0198765432

ISBN 0-07-222663-3

Publisher	**Proofreader**
Brandon A. Nordin	Susie Elkind
Vice President & Associate Publisher	**Computer Designer**
Scott Rogers	Lucie Ericksen
Acquisitions Editor	**Illustrators**
Marjorie McAneny	Lyssa Sieben-Wald
Project Editor	Michael Mueller
LeeAnn Pickrell	**Series Design**
Acquisitions Coordinator	Lyssa Wald
Tana Allen	Peter F. Hancik
Copy Editor	**Cover Design**
Jan Jue	Jeff Weeks

This book was composed with Corel VENTURA™ Publisher.

Dedication

This book is dedicated to Kellie: my wife, best friend, and favorite person in the world to watch DVDs with! This book is also dedicated to our family's new additions: our twins Jacob and Maya.

About the Author

Marc Saltzman has reported on the bourgeoning high-tech industry for the past six years as a freelance journalist, author, lecturer, consultant, and radio and TV personality. His specialties lie in video gaming, DVDs, computers, the Internet, telecommunications, digital music initiatives, and consumer electronics. One of the first journalists in the world to break open the MP3 phenomenon in late 1997 on CNN.com, Saltzman correctly predicted this controversial audio file format would revolutionize the recording industry.

Along with his weekly syndicated columns with Gannett News Service, Saltzman currently contributes to over two dozen prominent publications, reaching millions of readers each month: *USA Today/USAToday.com, CNN.com, LA Times, National Post, Globe and Mail Online, Maxim, Modern Maturity, Total Movie* magazine, *PC Gamer, Access* magazine, Inside Entertainment, and many more. He also serves as a regular on-air contributor to "Next @ CNN," a weekly hour-long technology program seen on CNN.

Saltzman lives in Richmond Hill, Ontario, Canada, with his wife and two children.

Table of Contents

Acknowledgments

A very special thank you goes out to the movie studios—namely Fox, Universal, DreamWorks, Disney/Buena Vista, Paramount, Warner Bros., New Line Cinema, MGM, Artisan, Lions Gate, HBO, Miramax, USA Entertainment, Anchor Bay Entertainment, LucasFilm, and Image Entertainment—who so graciously supplied us with all the materials and information we needed to put this exciting book together. Also, thank you to the wonderful acquisitions editor Margie McAneny for her sagely guidance and encouragement. I'd also like to thank the following folks at McGraw-Hill/Osborne—you wouldn't have this special book in your hands without their tireless work and savoir-faire: acquisitions coordinator Tana Allen, project editor LeeAnn Pickrell, copy editor Jan Jue, designers Lyssa Wald and Peter Hancik, art director Jeff Weeks, and marketing manager Kate Viotto. I'd also like to thank Marc Edward Heuck, "Movie Geek," for his foreword to the book.

Foreword

I didn't want to like DVD.

I had been a staunch laserdisc proponent since 1989, when I bought some unopened discs at a science fiction convention without even owning a player. Over the years, I ultimately bought three players, all second-hand, along with over 100 discs. I touted their impressive sound and proper matteing of widescreen movies to whoever would listen, and found myself often making VHS dubs of the better discs. (And I mastered the art of disguising side breaks on tape in the process too—almost seamless!)

Then came DVD, with its compact size and virtual duplication of all the features I had loved about laser. I was terrified. I had lived through the abandonment of Beta, 8-track, and the RCA CED disc format, not to mention the failure of the "digital compact cassette," and I was not about to replace my technology again. Besides, while DVD then was a new releases/blockbuster hit-driven medium, laser had reached a point where the great obscure films were finally getting released. I feared that it would easily take ten years for those kinds of films to get released in DVD, and that would depend on whether the format lasted that long. I gleefully searched magazines and web sites for flaws, and sure enough, those early DVDs did possess compression problems, lockups, awkward side breaks, and other manner of imperfections that I tried to scare potential buyers with.

Well, we all know who won this one, don't we? The technology improved, along with the presentations, and the added value elements that I loved of laser—trailers, stills, documentaries—multiplied exponentially. And while there are still a staggering number of titles still unavailable as of press time, I am amazed and gratified at the number of rarities that have been pressed onto those lil' silver platters. I still do not own as many DVDs as laserdiscs, but I'll be there soon enough. (I have kept all my lasers too, because the small problem that will always plague DVD is that certain laserdiscs I love and cherish will never be able to be duplicated in this format, thanks to rights lapses and lawyers. So if you got that set of Criterion James Bond titles with the Terence Young commentaries and the Wonder Bread ads, don't you dare sell them. They ain't coming back—ever.)

The subject of this book you're holding—the DVD Easter egg—I've often found myself having to defend to the uninitiated. Not all people possess a sense of adventure, and that often applies not only to the movies they watch, but also to how they watch them. "Huh? Widescreen composition? 5.1 vs. 2.0 sound? Languages, subtitles? Please, just fill my entire TV screen and make sure it's in English—is it too late to go back to VHS?" (And sadly, there are many craven individuals in the industry who will cater to that indifference.) So it is with the Easter egg. Even the cinephile often moans that they aren't interested in a hunting expedition when they watch DVD; if this feature is so funny, then announce it on the cover so I can find it easily. But that negates the whole joke. While some eggs are long and involved, such as the *Wizard of Oz*–themed *Rocky Horror Picture Show* option, some eggs seem somewhat superfluous; a clip of Udo Kier irritating the sound man on the *Suspiria* disc is hardly a selling point, but for those of us who love the movie, it's fun.

The Easter egg symbolizes the reward to the hardcore film fan like myself, the person who held out for the best quality presentation, and access to as many ancillary items about the film that can be had. When we love a film, we often want as much as we can on it, just like the Aerosmith fan who must own every magazine cover or alternate single mix. The Easter egg is that piece of ephemera that means nothing to the layman, but brings a smile to our face. And seeing as how before DVD, we often spent time hunting through video stores and "gray-market" dealers for the preferred version of our movies (enduring fifth generation bootlegs of *The Beyond*, frantically looking for first-issue tapes of *Slap Shot* before the reissued "music changed for home video" editions), the Easter egg is a fond reminder of those days. A safe way to look for more from that favorite film.

Granted, this book is simplifying the search for you. You won't have to press buttons at random to find the eggs anymore as I did before this book was written. But if you're like me, you spent enough time on the fruitless hunt. For once, it's nice to have a map to the treasure. Enjoy the spoils, we've earned them!

Marc Edward Heuck— "Movie Geek"
Comedy Central's BEAT THE GEEKS
Hollywood, California
August 2002

Introduction

If you've picked up this book, then chances are you've already jumped onto the DVD bandwagon.

And for good reason—those shiny little discs of joy offer countless advantages over those bulky VCR tapes collecting dust in the spare room: superior video and audio quality, bonus features, multiple caption/subtitle options, and the ability to play them on a computer as well as on a TV-based DVD player.

But, of course, you already know all that.

What you might not be aware of are the many secrets on the discs, known as "Easter eggs."

That's right—hundreds of today's DVD movies contain hidden surprises—most of which are revealed by punching in the correct combination of keys on the DVD remote. The Easter egg can be any number of fun extras: a blooper reel, deleted scenes, alternate endings, hidden trailers, musical scores, cartoons, interviews, video games, a personal message from the cast, and so forth.

Remember, we're not referring to the extra features listed on the back of the DVD box; these concealed gems reward those savvy and determined enough to find them. They're inserted at the request of the filmmaker or planted by the creators of the disc itself.

So, if they're such a secret, how do you find out about them?

You're holding it.

Introducing *DVD Confidential: Hundreds of Hidden Easter Eggs Revealed*!—your one-stop guide to the very finest in DVD Easter eggs.

Inside this book, you'll find countless eggs for DVD movies you may have in your collection, and of course, how to unlock them and what the payoff is. So be forewarned—consider this book the ultimate spoiler!

Keep in mind, some Easter eggs are easier to find than others, but we've decided to include a few of these not-so-hidden ones, too. If the goodies aren't listed on the back of the box, they're still considered "eggs"—and will be an added bonus for those buying or renting the flick.

So, whether you're a hardcore film fanatic, casual movie watcher, or somewhere in between, be sure to grab some popcorn, put your feet up, and turn the page to discover more than 350 eggs tucked away inside the best of today's and yesterday's DVDs!

The question remains: will you keep these secrets?

Alien

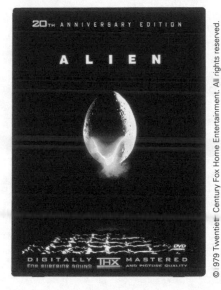

20th Century Fox

Released 1979

Directed by Ridley Scott

Starring Tom Skerritt, Sigourney Weaver, Veronica Cartwright, Harry Dean Stanton, John Hurt, Ian Holm, Yaphet Kotto

A*lien* is the first adventure in one of the most beloved sci-fi film series in history. The story begins as the crew of the spaceship *Nostromo* investigates a transmission from an "uninhabited" planet. However, something gets back on the ship with them and begins to attack crew members one by one. It's definitely one of those DVDs to watch with the lights off and the speakers cranked.

To access the eggs on this DVD (also found in the "Alien Legacy Box Set"), pop in the disc, and from the main menu, scroll down once and select "Extra Features." Once inside, scroll down to the bottom, and the acid pool on the floor will turn red. Press Enter to peruse a handful of interactive screens that outline the four stages of the alien's life cycle: "egg," "facehugger," "chestburster," and then "adult."

Now go back to the main menu, and highlight the words "Extra Features"— but don't press Enter just yet. Instead, tap the Left Arrow on the DVD remote, and the picture on the left side of the screen will now have a white border. Press Enter and the "camera" will swivel around to display the hidden credits for the making of this DVD.

Lastly, from the main menu again, highlight the words "Scene Selection," but don't hit Enter just yet. Press the Right Arrow, and the picture on the right of the screen will illuminate. Press Enter to view the *Nostromo* flight plan and some detailed (but of course, fictitious) information about each of the crew members. There are roughly four pages of dossier info and images for each of the seven crew members.

Great stuff!

Aliens: Special Edition

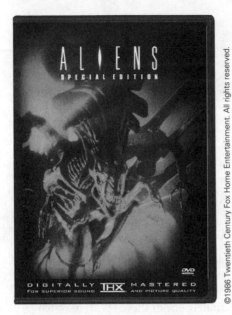

20th Century Fox

Released 1986

Directed by James Cameron

Starring Sigourney Weaver

The terror continues as Lt. Ellen Ripley (Sigourney Weaver)—the sole survivor from the last alien encounter—joins a crew of space marines to look into the disappearance of colonists on LV-426.

This "Special Edition" DVD (also found in the "Alien Legacy Box Set") features a couple of hidden surprises.

Pop in the disc and from the main menu, enter the "Extra Features" section. Once inside, scroll down to "Theatrical Trailers" to watch all the theatrical trailers to all four *Alien* films. These are not documented on the back of the DVD box.

Also, here's a small egg: while still in the "Extra Features" screen, scroll down five times until the vital signs display at the bottom of the screen has an orange border. Now press Enter to view the credits for the making of this disc.

Alien³

20th Century Fox

Released 1992

Directed by David Fincher

Starring Sigourney Weaver

Immediately following the events of *Aliens,* the spaceship carrying home Lieutenant Ripley (Sigourney Weaver) and other space marines crash lands on a prison planet. Ripley is left alone (without any weapons) to deal with the cause of the crash—a stowaway alien. As if this weren't stressful enough, Ripley soon discovers another horrifying truth about this beast's intentions.

From the main menu of this DVD, scroll up and enter the "Extra Features" submenu. Once inside, press Enter to select "The Making of Alien³ Featurette." Once this lengthy documentary is over, don't turn off the player just yet. A hidden *Alien³* trailer will begin— one that features scenes from the film that ended up on the cutting room floor!

Alien Resurrection

20th Century Fox

Released 1997

Directed by Jean-Pierre Jeunet

Starring Sigourney Weaver, Winona Ryder

You'd think Lieutenant Ripley (Sigourney Weaver) would choose another career path after three deadly alien encounters, yet she's back again. OK, to be fair, it's a cloned version of Ripley who was created to combat the creatures 200 years after the first three *Alien* adventures. She is joined by Annalee Call (Winona Ryder), a mechanic with a few surprises of her own.

Just as with the "Special Edition" *Aliens* DVD, undocumented theatrical trailers to all four *Alien* movies are planted on this disc.

Pop in the DVD, and from the main menu, select the "Extra Features" section. Along with the lengthy featurette on the making of this movie, you'll notice original theatrical trailers for *Alien, Aliens, Alien³*, and *Alien Resurrection*.

Top 10 Reasons Why DVDs Are Better than VHS

L et's face it—your bulky videocassettes are so 20th century. Other than the fact that most DVDs are not recordable (yet), they're far superior to videocassettes.

How are DVDs better than videotape? Let us count the ways:

1. Video—More than double the resolution of VHS.
2. Audio—Forget stereo speakers, we're talking 5.1 surround sound or greater.
3. Size—DVDs take up much less space.
4. Capacity—DVDs hold much more data than VHS tapes (i.e., extra features).
5. Cueing—No waiting to fast-forward or rewind tapes (remember that?).
6. Durability—DVDs last longer and have fewer parts to break.
7. Versatility—The same DVDs for your TV also work on computers with DVD-ROM drives.
8. Captions—Thanks to the optional subtitles, DVDs are great for those with impaired hearing.
9. Languages—Want to watch a movie in your mother tongue? Many DVDs offer alternate language tracks.
10. Extras—Easter eggs!

Almost Famous—Untitled: The Bootleg Cut

DreamWorks Pictures

Released 2000

Directed by Cameron Crowe

Starring Patrick Fugit, Billy Crudup, Jason Lee, Kate Hudson, Frances McDormand, Anna Paquin, Philip Seymour Hoffman, Fairuza Balk, Noah Taylor

In this somewhat autobiographical tale penned and directed by Cameron Crowe, a 15-year-old boy goes on tour with a rock band and writes about his adventures for *Rolling Stone* magazine.

This "Bootleg Cut" double-DVD features a few good eggs, too.

Insert the first disc, and from the main menu, scroll across and highlight the words "Special Features." Once inside this new menu screen, tap the Right Arrow on the DVD remote to highlight the words "Love Comes and Goes"—but don't press Enter just yet. Instead, tap the Up Arrow and the Polaroid picture on the right will turn red. Press Enter to watch an amusing outtake with Kate Hudson trying to get the name "Leslie" right, preceded by a lengthy explanation by Crowe.

Now go back to the main menu and select "Audio." Click over to the words "Commentary by Director Cameron Crowe," and then press the Right Arrow. The hole in the middle of the record will turn red; press Enter to be treated to an eerie outtake with actors Philip Seymour Hoffman and Patrick Fugit—but pay close attention to Crowe's explanation before the clip begins.

There's also a secret Easter egg on the second DVD: Pop in the disc, and from the main menu, select "Special Features." Now click on the "Cast" section, and once inside, choose the biography of Fairuza "Sapphire" Balk. Now press the Up Arrow, and the middle Polaroid picture of her will turn red. Press Enter to hear Crowe chat about working on this film, followed by an outtake of a deleted scene on the tour bus.

American Pie: Collector's Edition

Universal Pictures

Released 1999

Directed by Paul Weitz

Starring Jason Biggs, Chris Klein, Natasha Lyonne, Thomas Ian Nicholas, Tara Reid, Mena Suvari, Shannon Elizabeth, Alyson Hannigan, Seann William Scott, Eddie Kaye Thomas, Eugene Levy

This critically acclaimed comedy looks at the lives of four teenage boys who make a pact to lose their virginity by prom night. As expected, things don't go exactly as planned—for better or for worse.

From the main menu, select "Bonus Materials" and then enter the second page of these special features. Now click on "Recommendations" to watch three full, undocumented trailers to *Animal House, American Graffiti,* and *The Blues Brothers.* What a treat!

Here's another one—sit through the commercial for the *American Pie* soundtrack, and then enjoy the music video to Tonic's "You Wanted More," which should start immediately afterward.

These eggs do not exist on the "Ultimate Edition" of *American Pie.*

American Pie 2: Collector's Edition

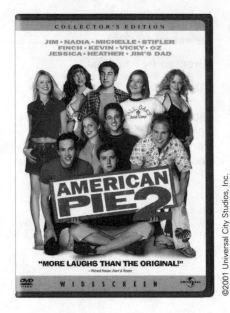

Universal Pictures

Released 2001

Directed by James B. Rogers

Starring Jason Biggs, Shannon Elizabeth, Alyson Hannigan, Chris Klein, Natasha Lyonne, Thomas Ian Nicholas, Tara Reid, Seann William Scott, Mena Suvari, Eddie Kaye Thomas, Eugene Levy

They're back! In this sequel to the hit comedy of '99, the gang has returned from a year away at college for an all-new summer adventure.

This "Collector's Edition" DVD features more than ten hours of extra features and a real Easter egg surprise.

From the main menu, select "Bonus Materials" and then enter the second page by clicking on the small arrow at the bottom of the screen. Now, instead of selecting one of these options, push the Up Arrow on the remote, and the words "Bonus Materials" will illuminate in red. Press Enter and let cast members Jason Biggs, Thomas Ian Nicholas, and Mena Suvari treat you to what you're after. You've been warned…

An American Werewolf in London: Collector's Edition

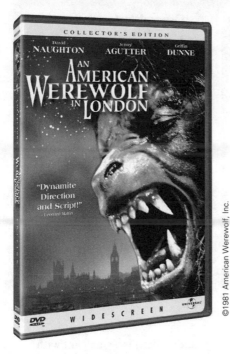

Universal Studios

Released 1981

Directed by John Landis

Starring David Naughton, Jenny Agutter, Griffin Dunne

This modern cult classic straddles horror and dark comedy, when two American students head to Europe on a backpacking expedition. Thanks to a vicious werewolf attack, one student ends up dead, and the other is hospitalized and suffers from monstrous nightmares.

Fans of the film can find a hidden trailer on this "Collector's Edition" DVD—if you know where to look, that is.

From the main menu, scroll up and press Enter over the words "Bonus Materials." Then select the word "Recommendations" on the lower right of the screen. On the second page is an image of the DVD for the classic film *The Wolf Man*. If you take a closer look, you'll notice a small video reel underneath it. Press Up Arrow on the remote, and the reel will turn white. Now press Enter to watch a rare trailer for the timeless black-and-white film.

Antz

SIGNATURE SELECTION

DreamWorks PICTURES and PDI

ANTZ

Every ant has his day.

WIDESCREEN

TM & ©1998 DreamWorks L.L.C., reprinted with premission by DreamWorks Animation.

DreamWorks Pictures

Released 1998

Directed by Eric Darnell, Tim Johnson

Starring Woody Allen, Dan Aykroyd, Anne Bancroft, Jane Curtin, Danny Glover, Gene Hackman, Jennifer Lopez, John Mahoney, Paul Mazursky, Grant Shaud, Sylvester Stallone, Sharon Stone, Christopher Walken

In this animated adventure, Z (voice of Woody Allen) is a small ant with some big ideas—one of which is to land Princess Bala (voice of Sharon Stone) as his girlfriend. He convinces his soldier buddy Weaver (voice of Sylvester Stallone) to switch places with him to get closer to her, and his mundane life takes a wild turn.

This DVD contains a number of special features and a little-known egg, too.

From the main menu, go to the "Special Features" screen. If you look closely, you'll see a small white DreamWorks logo on the bottom leaf (along the left portion of the screen). To access it, press the Left Arrow followed by the Down Arrow, and the leaf should now be highlighted.

Press Enter to watch an enjoyable animated credits screen for this DVD of *Antz,* playing to the song "I Can See Clearly Now."

Apollo 13: Collector's Edition

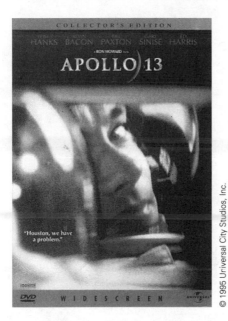

Universal Studios

Released 1995

Directed by Ron Howard

Starring Tom Hanks, Kevin Bacon, Bill Paxton, Gary Sinise, Ed Harris

© 1995 Universal City Studios, Inc.

"Houston, we have a problem."

Apollo 13 is based on a true story chronicling the ill-fated journey of a "routine space flight" to the moon in 1970. The three astronauts on board—Jim Lovell, Fred Haise, and Jack Swigert, as played by Tom Hanks, Bill Paxton, and Kevin Bacon, respectively—must come to grips with their near-impossible task of making it back home alive.

Directed by Ron Howard, *Apollo 13* was one of the more critically acclaimed and commercially successful films of 1995.

As a special—and secret—treat, the entire musical score to the film is hidden on this disc (and in Dolby Digital!).

Here's how to access it—do nothing!

Insert the DVD and let the main menu screen load, and you can now toggle between each of the classical audio tracks by pressing the right and left Skip buttons on the remote. Enjoy!

Atlantis: The Lost Empire, Collector's Edition

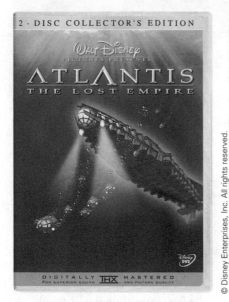

Walt Disney Pictures

Released 2001

Directed by Gary Trousdale, Kirk Wise

Starring Michael J. Fox

In this animated adventure set in the year 1914, Milo Thatch (voice of Michael J. Fox) is a young adventurer who joins a brave group of explorers to find the lost continent of Atlantis.

This two-disc "Collector's Edition" DVD is jam-packed with extra features including visual commentaries, a "DisneyPedia," deleted scenes, animation production featurettes, and much more.

With all that work, the team responsible for this DVD should be acknowledged, no? The Easter egg will unlock the credits screen.

Insert the second disc, dubbed "Supplemental Features," and from the main menu, select the word "Explore." Once inside, scroll down to highlight the section "Animation Production," but don't press Enter just yet. Instead, press the Right Arrow, and the words "DVD Credits" will appear. Now press Enter to read the credits on the making of this double-disc set.

Austin Powers: International Man of Mystery

New Line Cinema

Released 1997

Directed by Jay Roach

Starring Mike Myers, Elizabeth Hurley

O h, behave!

This groovy film stars Mike Myers as Austin Powers, a secret agent frozen in the '60s and thawed back into action in the '90s to battle his archenemy, Dr. Evil (also played by Myers). Can Powers and his sexy sidekick, Ms. Kensington (Elizabeth Hurley), manage to stop Dr. Evil's plot to control the world?

Pop in either side of the DVD ("Standard" or Widescreen"), and from the main menu, select "Extra Stuff." Now scroll down four times, select "The Cast," and then choose "Mimi Rogers." On the second page of her biography is a pink star beside the *Lost in Space* tab. Select it and press Enter to watch a lengthy trailer to the sci-fi film. On the same bio screen, look at the bottom and you'll find a video clip of Rogers in *Monkey Trouble;* there's also a third video clip of her in *The Rapture* on the last page of her biography.

While still inside the "The Cast" section, select Elizabeth Hurley and scroll through her bio to watch a scene of her in *Dangerous Ground*.

Another video clip, for the film *Wide Sargasso Sea,* can be found in Michael York's biography.

The Best Movie Sequels

We all know most movie sequels don't match the charm of their predecessors. The following dozen films are exceptions to the rule (not listed in any particular order):

1. The Godfather: Part II
2. Star Wars: Episode V—The Empire Strikes Back
3. Aliens
4. Toy Story 2
5. The Road Warrior (Mad Max 2)
6. The Bride of Frankenstein
7. Evil Dead II
8. American Pie 2
9. From Russia With Love
10. Terminator 2
11. Austin Powers: The Spy Who Shagged Me
12. Indiana Jones and the Last Crusade

Austin Powers: The Spy Who Shagged Me

New Line Cinema

Released 1999

Directed by Jay Roach

Starring Mike Myers, Heather Graham

Shagalicious, baby! This follow-up to the 1997 James Bond spoof (*Austin Powers: International Man of Mystery*) now shines the spotlight on Dr. Evil (Mike Myers) as he uses a time machine to go back to 1969 to drain Austin Powers (also Mike Myers) of his "mojo." Powers also heads back in time with the aid of his sexy sidekick Felicity Shagwell (Heather Graham). Dr. Evil's sidekick is a clone of himself—but about one eighth his size—known as "Mini Me" (Verne Troyer).

From the main menu—where an animated Powers dances and dishes out his oh-so-sexy lines such as "Click it—you're making me randy, baby"— select the "Special Features" option.

Don't touch anything—let Austin continue with his silly antics. After about 30 seconds, Dr. Evil's phallic spaceship will appear, soaring from the bottom of the screen up to the top, leaving behind a large *E* in the middle of the screen. Navigate to it and press Enter once the *E* turns red.

Press Enter and the *E* will turn green. The screen will then flip to the hidden "Dr. Evil's Special Features" page, which includes four special sections: the lengthy "Comedy Central's Canned Ham: The Dr. Evil Story" (a mock documentary, or "mocumentary"!), two music video-esque excerpts from the film ("What if God Was One of Us" and "Just the Two of Us," both performed by Dr. Evil and Mini-Me), and "Classic Evil Schemes Gone Awry," a humorous look at foiled attempts at killing the protagonist in classic films.

Also, you may notice the small New Line Cinema logo underneath "Special Features." Scroll down and select this to be taken to numerous pages from companies responsible for the making of this disc.

Basic Instinct: Special Edition

Artisan Entertainment

Released 1992

Directed by Paul Verhoeven

Starring Michael Douglas, Sharon Stone

Detective Nick Curran (Michael Douglas) begins investigating the kinky murder of a rock star and discovers he was killed in the same fashion as described in a novel by the deceased musician's seductive girlfriend, Catherine Tramell (Sharon Stone). This modern-day whodunit introduces new plot twists throughout the film, and thus, keeps the audience guessing on the killer's identity.

Artisan's "Special Edition" of this DVD features a few eggs—and a promotional ice-pick pen, as well!

Scroll down and select the "Special Features" section. Press the Right Arrow once to illuminate the ice pick. Press Enter and the ice pick will turn red. Now viewers can watch a lengthy rehearsal sequence with Sharon Stone—including the infamous interrogation and lie detector scenes, and two others.

Now enter the "Setup" area of the DVD, press the Right Arrow on the remote three times, and the ice pick will turn yellow. Press Enter to view more rehearsal footage—this time from Jeanne Tripplehorn, who plays Dr. Elisabeth Garner in the film.

Lastly, select the "JVC" logo on the bottom left of the "Setup" screen (turning it from red to yellow), and then press Enter to watch a commercial for JVC products.

Battlefield Earth

Warner Bros.

Released 2000

Directed by Roger Christian

Starring John Travolta, Barry Pepper, Forest Whitaker

In the year 3000, Earth is under attack from an alien race known as the Psychlos, led by the vicious alien security chief, Terl (John Travolta). Humans, of course, won't take this attempt at global domination lying down, so a rebel group lead by Jonnie Goodboy Tyler (Barry Pepper) prepares to fight back.

From the DVD's main menu, head to the section "Special Features." Once inside, tap the Right Arrow on the DVD remote, and a blue symbol will appear over the deadly machine in the picture. Press Enter to watch some never-before-released makeup work done on the actors.

While back in the "Special Features" page, click "Continue" to enter the second page of bonus materials. Now press the Right Arrow, and that same blue symbol will appear over the pyramid. Press Enter for more behind-the-scenes footage of a group of actors running through the town.

Head back to the second page of "Special Features," and choose the last option: "Cast & Crew." Try the same thing again by pressing the Right Arrow, and the blue symbol will appear over the image. Press Enter to watch some rehearsal stunt work.

Now go back to the main menu and enter the "Languages" submenu. Press the Right Arrow to watch even more stunt rehearsals.

The Beach

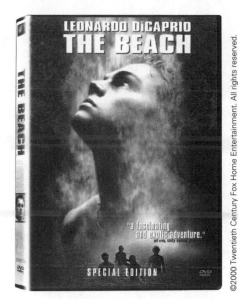

20th Century Fox

Released 2000

Directed by Danny Boyle

Starring Leonardo DiCaprio, Tilda Swinton, Virginie Ledoyen, Guillaume Canet, Robert Carlyle

The adventurous Richard (Leonardo DiCaprio) is an American backpacker who travels alone to Thailand and convinces a young French couple to join him on a journey to find an island paradise.

The DVD features audio commentary by the film's director, nine deleted scenes, a storyboard gallery, a music video, and an undocumented Easter egg.

From the main menu, scroll across three times and select the word "Features." Once inside, scroll down and press Enter over the "Cast & Crew" option.

Now select the page for actor "Robert Carlyle," and if you press the Left Arrow while reading his biography, his picture on the left side of the screen will illuminate in red. Press Enter to watch the full trailer for *The Full Monty*, which also stars Carlyle.

The Beastmaster

Anchor Bay Entertainment

Released 1982

Directed by Don Coscarelli

Starring Marc Singer, Tanya Roberts, Rip Torn, John Amos

Don Coscarelli's *The Beastmaster* is a fantasy cult classic about a warrior, Dar (Marc Singer), on a journey to avenge his parent's murder. He is helped by a skilled hunter, Seth (John Amos); a beautiful slave girl, Kiri (Tanya Roberts); and the cunning ability to communicate with animals. Veteran actor Rip Torn plays the malevolent priest Maax—the one responsible for the slaughter of Dar's family.

Select "Extras" from the main menu, and you'll notice new areas to explore, such as behind-the-scenes footage, product art, posters, and still galleries. Instead of choosing one of these options, press the Right Arrow a few times to scroll down the list of options. After "Main Menu," a yellow circle will appear.

Press Enter and the circle will turn into an eye and will then cut to unreleased footage including five minutes of alternate love scenes between Dar and Kiri (with partial nudity), and in the company of a restless black tiger.

The Beatles: Yellow Submarine

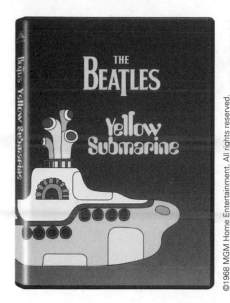

MGM

Released 1968

Directed by George Dunning

Starring John Lennon, Paul McCartney, George Harrison, Ringo Starr

This visionary cartoon tells the tale of the Fab Four as they set sail and search for the music-hating Blue Meanies, so they can put an end to the Meanies' evil reign over the citizens of Pepperland.

The soundtrack features many of The Beatles' beloved songs, including "All You Need Is Love," "Sgt. Pepper's Lonely Hearts Club Band," and, of course, "Yellow Submarine."

A movie as surreal as this was made for hidden eggs, and thankfully, there are a number of them on the DVD.

From the disc's main menu, press the Up Arrow, and George Harrison looking out of the porthole will turn purple. Press Enter to hear an audio clip from him in the movie. The same can be done by navigating with the Right Arrow and Left Arrow buttons to select other members of the band.

You can also highlight in purple four empty portholes by moving over them using the remote. Press Enter to hear music clips and to view cartoon characters and animation.

Try moving the remote over other areas around and on the submarine, and you'll find 14 eggs.

Bedazzled: Special Edition

20th Century Fox

Released 2000

Directed by Harold Ramis

Starring Brendan Fraser, Elizabeth Hurley

It's hard to find a "hotter" devil than Elizabeth Hurley in this entertaining remake about a hapless computer technician, Elliot Richards (Brendan Fraser), who falls for the Princess of Darkness' seductive ways. Richards agrees to sell his soul for seven wishes, and naturally, a few unexpected strings are attached.

If you want to see one of Richards' wishes that didn't make it to the final version of the film, you'll need to unlock the Easter egg on this devilish comedy.

Pop in the DVD, and from the main menu, go to the "Special Features" area, and then select "More"' to enter the second page.

Press the Right Arrow and a little red devil will appear on the devil's left shoulder. Press Enter and sit back to watch a risqué ten-minute deleted scene in which Richards becomes a drug-addicted rock star. (Note: Due to its mature content, this segment is not for kids.)

Behind Enemy Lines

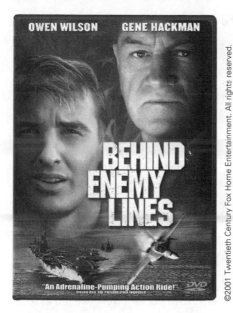

20th Century Fox

Released 2001

Directed by John Moore

Starring Gene Hackman, Owen Wilson

U.S. Navy pilot Chris Burnett (Owen Wilson) is shot down during a recon mission over Bosnia and must fight to stay alive until his commanding officer Leslie Reigart (Gene Hackman) can launch a renegade rescue mission—against strict NATO orders.

Allegedly, *Behind Enemy Lines* is the first film to feature the U.S. Navy's new F/A-18E/F Super Hornet.

From the main menu of this DVD, scroll down and select the "Special Features" section, and then choose the "Pre-Vis Ejection Sequence."

Now press the Up Arrow on the remote, and a red star will appear on the screen. Press Enter to watch a hidden (and humorous) outtake with actor Wilson on the back of a pickup truck.

Being John Malkovich

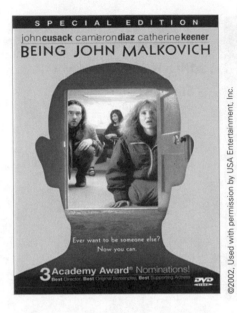

USA Films/Universal Pictures

Released 1999

Directed by Spike Jonze

Starring John Cusack, Cameron Diaz, Catherine Keener, Orson Bean, Mary Kay Place, John Malkovich

In this refreshingly unique film, Craig Schwartz (John Cusack) is a struggling street puppeteer who decides to take a job as a filing clerk to make more money. He soon discovers a secret door, which serves as a portal into the brain of actor John Malkovich (played in the film by John Malkovich). Strange, but highly entertaining.

The eggs on this DVD aren't as strange as the film—nor are they too hard to find—but they're rewarding nonetheless.

On the DVD, enter the "Language Selection" section from the main menu and then don't press anything. Instead, turn up the volume, and listen to an entire song by Björk, entitled "Amphibian."

More soundtrack music from the film can be heard throughout these menu screens, such as the instrumental track on the "Special Features" page.

Now go to the second page of the "Special Features" section, and one of the choices will be "Don't enter here, there is nothing here." If you're curious, press Enter over these words to be taken to a new screen that says "There is nothing here, press enter to return."

Well, what did you expect?

Big Trouble in Little China

20th Century Fox

Released 1986

Directed by John Carpenter

Starring Kurt Russell, Kim Cattrall

This supernatural action flick stars an unlikely hero—truck driver Jack Burton (Kurt Russell)—as he helps save his friend's fiancée, Gracie Law (Kim Cattrall), from an evil Chinatown sorcerer. Of course, he's also out to rescue his beloved truck!

Insert the second DVD and from the main menu, select the word "More," which takes you to the second page of bonus materials. Once here, scroll over to "Cast & Crew" and press Enter. Now press the Left Arrow, and you'll notice a yellow outline surrounding actor James Hong. Press Enter to read his filmography. Keep pressing the Right Arrow to access the filmography for the other cast and crew members.

Now go to the third page of "Special Features" (by pressing "More" again), and scroll down to highlight the words "Richard Edlund Interview." Instead of pressing Enter, tap the Right Arrow and a pair of yellow eyes will appear on the right side of the screen. Press Enter to be taken to a "Summer 1986" screen with three movie trailers for you to enjoy: *Aliens, Big Trouble in Little China,* and *The Fly*.

Now go back to the "Special Features" menu and select "DVD Production Credits" at the bottom of the screen. Once inside, click Enter to scroll through the pages of credits, and eventually you'll be treated to eight screen shots from the "Big Trouble in Little China" Commodore 64 computer game. Man, have graphics changed!

The Blair Witch Project

Artisan

Released 1999

Directed by Daniel Myrick, Eduardo Sánchez

Starring Heather Donahue, Michael Williams, Joshua Leonard

You remember the premise behind this mega-successful independent horror film: in October of 1994, three student filmmakers disappeared in the woods near Burkittsville, Maryland, while shooting a documentary… a year later their footage was found.

Pop in the DVD and from the main menu, head to the section "Special Features" (the last option on the screen). Now, instead of selecting from this list, press the Right Arrow on the DVD remote, and a large yellow Blair Witch stick figure will appear in the bottom-right corner of the screen.

Press Enter to watch a trailer for *The Blair Witch Project,* two extra teaser trailers for the film, and a bonus trailer for Stephen King's *The Stand,* a DVD featuring the six-hour made-for-TV movie.

Blair Witch 2: The Book of Shadows

Artisan Entertainment

Released 2000

Directed by Joe Berlinger

Starring Kim Director, Jeffrey Donovan, Erica Leerhsen, Tristine Skyler, Stephen Barker Turner

Four young fans of the original Blair Witch movie decide to visit Burkittsville, Maryland, and spend the night in creepy Rustin Parr house. The next day, the college students realize the footage they shot on camera doesn't exactly gel with their memory from the night before.

The DVD is chock-full of hidden features.

From the main menu, select "Scene Index" and press Enter. Tap the Right Arrow to access the first of many rune symbols peppered throughout this DVD, giving more insight into the Blair Witch mythology. Press Enter to read up on the significance of this rune.

Additional runes can be found by entering the "Chapters 1–4" area of the "Scene Index" section (here, press the Left Arrow on the remote), and another rune is found in the "Audio Features" section by pressing the Right Arrow three times.

More can be found in the "DVD-ROM Materials" section, the "Production Notes" area, and the "Cast & Crew" pages.

There's another egg. Visit the "Audio Features" section, and once inside, highlight the "Priority Records" tab and press Enter to unlock a secret live video featuring the band GodHead.

Lastly, while it's not quite an Easter egg, *Blair Witch 2: The Book of Shadows* is the first disc to deliver a DVD movie on one side and a full music CD on the other side (which can be played in any CD player).

Enjoy!

Blow

New Line Cinema

Released 2001

Directed by Ted Demme

Starring Johnny Depp, Penélope Cruz

In this true story, George Jung (Johnny Depp) becomes the largest importer of Columbian cocaine to the United States in the '70s and '80s. This film chronicles the rise and fall of his career and examines Jung's relationship with drug lord Pablo Escobar (Cliff Curtis) and his wife, Mirtha (Penélope Cruz).

On this DVD, scroll down to the bottom over the words "Need Help?" but don't press Enter just yet. Instead, press the Right Arrow, and a New Line Cinema "Infinifilm" logo will appear on the lower-right corner of the screen.

Press Enter for ten pages of DVD credits. Yes, it takes that many people to create a good DVD these days!

Blue Velvet: Special Edition

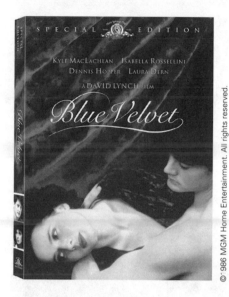

MGM

Released 1986

Directed by David Lynch

Starring Kyle MacLachlan, Isabella Rossellini, Dennis Hopper, Laura Dern

Leave it to David Lynch to dig below the surface of a seemingly quiet American town and expose a dark and disturbing underworld.

On this "Special Edition" DVD, some Easter eggs also lie below the surface.

From the main menu, scroll down, and a blue picket fence will appear over a video clip at the bottom of the screen. Press Enter and then all the video clips on the main menu page will change to four new ones. Scroll down once again and a blue bird will appear over the second video clip. Press Enter and it'll turn red just before launching a behind-the-scenes interview on how the filmmakers found the robin for the movie. Interesting tale!

Now, from the main menu, select "Special Features" and use the remote to scroll up once. The word "Special" in "Special Features" will turn red. Press Enter to hear David Lynch divulge his unhealthy eating habits.

Also from the "Special Features" menu, select the first entry, "Documentary: The Mysteries of Love." Instead of selecting from this list of chapters, press the Up Arrow, and the words "Mysteries of Love" will turn red. Now press Enter to watch an interview clip featuring actress Isabella Rossellini, who talks about the accusations of Lynch being a misogynist.

But wait—there's one more.

From the main menu, choose the "Scene Selections" section, and by pressing the Left Arrow or Right Arrow, you'll see a blue ear appear in between sections 3 and 4. Press Enter for additional interview footage, this time with Kyle MacLachlan, who chats about the origins of his silly "Chicken Walk" scene (also shown here).

Boogie Nights: Special Edition

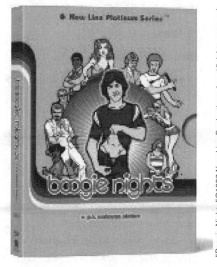

New Line Cinema

Released 1997

Directed by Paul Thomas Anderson

Starring Mark Wahlberg, Julianne Moore, Burt Reynolds, Don Cheadle, John C. Reilly, William H. Macy, Heather Graham, Nicole Parker, Philip Seymour Hoffman

It's the late 1970s and porn director Jack Horner (Burt Reynolds) discovers an aspiring actor, Eddie Adams (Mark Wahlberg), and transforms him into Dirk Diggler. Thanks to Diggler's "gift" and determination, he becomes a star in the adult-film industry—but of course, fame and fortune have a price, as Adams soon realizes.

Pop in the first disc from this "Special Edition" set, and from the main menu, select the "Setup" screen and then choose "Color Bars." This will take you to those familiar TV color bars to adjust your set, but wait 15 seconds or so, and you'll be treated to an outtake of the adult awards ceremony. Actor Robert Ridgely (who plays "Colonel James" in the movie) apparently ad-libbed much of this hilarious sequence.

After this clip, be forewarned—there's a few minutes of the "Diggler" in the raw with his, er, prosthetic penis. (Note: This is likely not Wahlberg, as the body's face is cut off from view in this extended version of the memorable scene from the movie.)

Now put in the second DVD, scroll over to the small black New Line Cinema logo, and press Enter. This will take you to the DVD credits for this two-disc set.

Bowfinger

Universal Studios

Released 1999

Directed by Frank Oz

Starring Steve Martin, Eddie Murphy, Heather Graham

© 1999 Universal City Studios, Inc.

Bobby Bowfinger (Steve Martin), a down-and-out movie director, must find a way to get Hollywood's biggest celebrity, Kit Ramsey (Eddie Murphy), to star, against his wishes, in a film. How does he achieve this? With the help of Kit's nerdy look-alike brother, Jiff (Eddie Murphy), and an ambitious wannabe, Daisy (Heather Graham).

Thankfully, this DVD isn't as low budget as *Cubby Rain,* the film they're making in *Bowfinger.* While not quite an Easter egg, a handful of undocumented trailers to other Universal films appear on this DVD.

From the main menu, select "Bonus Materials," click Enter to access the second page, and scroll down to select "Recommendations."

Over these next two pages, there are trailers to *Liar Liar, The Nutty Professor,* and *EDtv.*

But wait—there's one more.

Go back to the "Recommendations" page, and scroll up to "Universal Showcase" to watch a dramatic movie trailer to *Hurricane* starring Denzel Washington as Rubin "Hurricane" Carter.

The Bride of Frankenstein

© 1935 Universal Pictures Corporation.

Universal Studios

Released 1935

Directed by James Whale

Starring Boris Karloff, Colin Clive, Ernest Thesiger

S he's alive!

One of the most acclaimed horror classics in movie-making history (and a sequel to *Frankenstein*, released four years earlier), this bizarre tale returns Dr. Frankenstein (Colin Clive) as the scientist who must create a mate for everyone's favorite square-headed monster, Frankenstein (Boris Karloff).

Their courtship doesn't go quite as planned.

On the DVD, select "Bonus Materials" from the main menu, and then scroll down to select "Cast & Filmmakers" (second choice from the bottom).

Select the first entry—"Boris Karloff as The Monster"—and scroll to the seventh page using the Right Arrow on the remote. You'll notice there's a small word "Preview" beside "Frankenstein." Press Up Arrow on the remote until the word turns green, and then press Enter to watch a special treat—the original 1931 trailer to the film *Frankenstein*.

The same exciting trailer can be seen on the fourth page under director James Whales' biography/filmography, also in the "Cast & Filmmakers" section.

Bring It On

Universal Pictures

Released 2000

Directed by Peyton Reed

Starring Kirsten Dunst, Eliza Dushku, Jesse Bradford, Gabrielle Union

The Rancho Carne High School cheerleading team thought they'd snag the national championships once again—that is, until newly elected team captain Torrance Shipman (Kirsten Dunst) discovers their routine was lifted from a hot hip-hop squad across town. With little time to spare, the cheerleaders need to come up with some new moves for the competition.

From the disc's main menu, scroll over to "Languages" and press Enter. On this new screen, continuously press the Right Arrow on the remote until the yellow cheerleading cone in the lower-right corner of the screen turns red.

Now press Enter and the film's director, Peyton Reed, will appear with this humorous message: "Hey! You found it! The Easter egg! You probably were expecting a really beautiful cheerleader but instead you got me—a skinny, pathetic director. Nice job!"

The 'Burbs

Universal Studios

Released 1989

Directed by Joe Dante

Starring Tom Hanks, Bruce Dern, Carrie Fisher

Tom Hanks portrays suburbanite Ray Peterson, whose vacation- at-home goes awry when he and his wacky neighbors—a paranoid ex-soldier, a hefty busybody, and a spaced-out teenager—begin to investigate the strange happenings next door at Dr. Klopek's residence. Needless to say, Peterson's vacation proves to be anything but relaxing.

Here's a bit o' trivia: in the Klopek's house, the sled is named "Rosebud," an obvious nod to *Citizen Kane*, and their dog is named "Landru," a likely reference to Henri "Bluebeard" Landru, the infamous French serial killer.

The DVD for this suspenseful comedy has an undocumented alternate ending—from the main menu, select "Bonus Materials" and then select the "Alternate Ending" option at the top of the screen.

Enjoy this never-before-released ten-minute clip as Peterson is saved from Dr. Werner Klopek (Henry Gibson) before the ambulance takes off.

Carrie

MGM

Released 1976

Directed by Brian De Palma

Starring Sissy Spacek, John Travolta, Piper Laurie

"If *The Exorcist* made you shudder, *Carrie* will make you scream" was one of the taglines for this chilling horror flick about a teenage outcast with special powers. She gets pushed too far on prom night, and as you can imagine, the evening turns into a, er, bloody mess.

Carrie was Stephen King's first novel-turned-film in 1976, followed by *Salem's Lot* in 1979 (a made-for-TV movie) and *The Shining* in 1980.

If you have the guts to watch this nail-biting thriller all the way through, perhaps you'll also have the stomach for a little-known image at the very end?

Let the credits roll (or fast forward through them), and after the screen goes black, you'll be treated to a still shot of a bloody Carrie with her mom peeking behind the door...

Did You Know?

The "blood" that was dumped on Carrie White (Sissy Spacek) in the climatic prom scene was actually gallons of corn syrup and food coloring.

Casablanca

Warner Bros.

Released 1942

Directed by Michael Curtiz

Starring Humphrey Bogart,
Ingrid Bergman, Paul Henreid

This film tells the tale of an exiled American, Rick Blaine (Humphrey Bogart), who runs the hottest nightclub in Casablanca during World War II. Ingrid Bergman stars as Ilsa Lund, Blaine's ex-lover who deserted him in Paris. She comes to the nightclub as the companion of an underground leader, Victor Laszlo (Paul Henreid)—with Germans on their tail.

Since its original theatrical release in 1942, the film spawned countless lousy Bogart impressions for generations to come. Here's looking at you, kid.

Although the Easter eggs in this classic film aren't too hard to find, they are indeed undocumented extras, and a special treat, too.

From the main menu of the movie, select the "Special Features" page. You'll find eight movie trailers: *The Petrified Forest, High Sierra, The Maltese Falcon, Passage to Marseille, To Have and Have Not, The Big Sleep, Treasure of the Sierra Madre,* and *Key Largo.*

Sit back and enjoy.

Cast Away

20th Century Fox

Released 2000

Directed by Robert Zemeckis

Starring Tom Hanks

FedEx systems engineer Chuck Noland (Tom Hanks) washes up on a deserted island after a harrowing plane crash. With hope, determination, and an instinct for survival, Noland overcomes physical and emotional adversities and plans his escape off the island.

Insert the second (that is, "Supplemental") disc, and then select "Video and Stills Galleries" from the main menu. Use the remote to scroll down to the words "Raft Escape"—but instead of pressing Enter—tap the Left Arrow on the remote, and a set of yellow and blue wings will appear toward the left of the screen. Now press Enter.

As the text explains on this page, on March 13, 2001, director Robert Zemeckis participated in a Q&A at the USC School of Cinema and Television. One student asked the director what was in the unopened FedEx package Noland carried around with him throughout the movie. If you press "Play," you'll hear his response, followed by laughter and applause.

Did You Know?

The name of the volleyball in the film is "Wilson"—that's also the last name of Tom Hanks' wife, actress Rita Wilson.

On an airplane Tom Hanks' character (Chuck Noland) is served a can of Dr Pepper. That particular soda also happens to be the drink of choice for Hanks' character in *Forrest Gump*.

Cats & Dogs

Warner Bros.

Released 2001

Directed by Lawrence Guterman

Starring Jeff Goldblum, Elizabeth Perkins, Alexander Pollock

In this unlikely "tail," a young beagle named Lou is out to stop a cunning cat from enslaving all of humanity.

If you get your paws on this DVD, select the word "Cats" from the main menu, and then scroll down four times until a red block at the bottom of the screen turns white. Press Enter to play a hidden trivia game. You're asked three questions (and the correct answer for each is "Cats"), prompting a cute graphic that says "Congratulations: Proceed to Cat Headquarters."

Here's another egg: While still in the "Cats" portion of the DVD, select "Special Features" and then press the Down Arrow on the remote until the cat's prickly toy is highlighted on the left of the screen. Press Enter to watch Mr. Tinkles' screen tests for other (fake) films including parodies of *Apocalypse Now, The Terminator, The Sixth Sense,* and *Forrest Gump.* Wait to the very end for a cute surprise!

On the second page of "Special Features," scroll down three times until the image of the cat turns red. Press Enter to watch some "frisky" clips from *Cats & Dogs.*

Now eject the DVD and start it again, this time choosing "Dogs" from the main menu. Press the Down Arrow four times, and a white block at the bottom of the screen will turn blue. Press Enter and play this trivia game, with all the answers being "Dog," prompting another "Congratulations!" screen with a graphic.

Now select "Special Features" and scroll down three times until the tube in the middle of the screen turns pale blue. Press Enter to enjoy some concept sketches for the film.

Lastly, go to the second "Special Features" page, and scroll down three times until the emblem turns another color. Now press Enter to watch some "doggone" clips from the film.

Top Films as Chosen by You

According to voters at the Internet Movie Database (www.imdb.com), one of the most popular destinations on the Internet for movie lovers, the top 20 movies of all time are as follows:

1. The Godfather
2. The Shawshank Redemption
3. The Godfather: Part II
4. The Lord of the Rings: The Fellowship of the Ring
5. Citizen Kane
6. Schindler's List
7. Casablanca
8. Shichinin no samurai
9. Star Wars
10. Memento
11. Dr. Strangelove or: How I Learned to Stop Worrying and Love the Bomb
12. Le Fabuleux destin d'Amélie Poulain
13. One Flew Over the Cuckoo's Nest
14. Rear Window
15. Usual Suspects
16. Raiders of the Lost Ark
17. Star Wars: Episode V—The Empire Strikes Back
18. Psycho
19. Pulp Fiction
20. North by Northwest

Chasing Amy: The Criterion Collection

Miramax/Buena Vista Home Entertainment

Released 1997

Directed by Kevin Smith

Starring Ben Affleck, Joey Lauren Adams, Jason Lee, Dwight Ewell, Jason Mewes, Kevin Smith

Comic-book artist Holden McNeil (Ben Affleck) falls in love with fellow artist (and lesbian) Alyssa Jones (Joey Lauren Adams), threatening their friendship and his work relationship with his business partner, Banky Edwards (Jason Lee).

This special edition "Criterion Collection" DVD houses a number of extras designed for fans of Kevin Smith's film.

From the disc's main menu, the last option on this screen is "Color Bars"—you know, the color-bar test pattern as seen on TV. Before the color bars start, listen as Smith, Affleck, Scott Mosier, and Jason Mewes joke around, and then again during the color bars, and again at the end of them.

Typical silliness from Kevin Smith and company!

Chicken Run

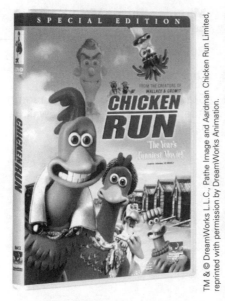

DreamWorks Pictures

Released 2000

Directed by Peter Lord, Nick Park

Starring Mel Gibson, Julia Sawalha, Lynn Ferguson, Jane Horrocks, Phil Daniels, Timothy Spall, Tony Haygarth, Miranda Richardson, Imelda Staunton, Benjamin Whitrow

This hilarious animated film chronicles the lives of confined chickens who decide to fly the coup with the help of a smooth-talking American rooster, Rocky Rhodes (Mel Gibson).

You'll find a dozen eggs in *Chicken Run* (fitting, huh?).

These cracked-egg images—when found and accessed on this DVD—reveal some neat facts about the feature film.

For example, from the main menu, select the "Audio" option, scroll down to the words "2.0 Digital Surround," but don't press Enter. Instead, press the Down Arrow again, and an orange cracked egg will appear in the middle of the screen. Press Enter to read a random fun fact.

One of the factoids says: "There are 100 stages in the process of making an average chicken. Each stage is divided into the following processes: body, armature, fluffles (feathers), legs, head, beak, comb, cowl, wings, tail, necklace, color and eyes."

There are 11 other orange and green eggs hidden elsewhere on these DVD menus—see how many you can find.

You can find them here:

- Audio menu—below "2.0 Dolby Digital"
- Subtitles menu—above "Main Menu"
- Special Features menu—above "Main Menu"
- Trailers and TV Spots menu—to the right of "TV Spot"
- Production Notes menu—on page 5 beside Back icon
- Mel Gibson menu in Cast section—above word "Bios"
- Tony Haygarth menu in Cast section—page 2, above "Bios"
- Jane Horrocks menu in Cast section—page 2, by Back icon
- Imelda Staunton menu in Cast section—above "Bios"
- Loyd Price menu in Crew section—page 2, by Back icon
- Dave Alex Riddett in Crew section—above "Bios"
- Scene Index—between scenes 17 and 18

If you want to read all 12 factoids without trying to find all the eggs, simply reenter eggs you've found (in the Audio submenu, for example), and each factoid should be randomly generated, thus different. Eventually, you'll read all dozen.

Another fun thing to do on this DVD: Click the "Panic Button" icon from the main menu and "Special Features" menu to watch several different clips of the hens screaming!

Lastly, the "Sneak Preview" inside the "Trailer and TV Spots" menu is of DreamWorks' blockbuster *Shrek*.

Citizen Kane

Warner Bros.

Released 1941

Directed by Orson Welles

Starring Joseph Cotten, Dorothy Comingore, Agnes Moorehead, George Coulouris, Ruth Warrick, Ray Collins

In Orson Welles' masterpiece, which was nominated for a Best Picture award in 1942 (but lost out to *How Green Was My Valley*), multimillionaire newspaper tycoon Charles Foster Kane dies alone, uttering a single word, "Rosebud." This film chronicles the sensational life of Kane, examines his personal and professional affairs, and sheds light on the meaning of his dying word.

On the DVD, visit the "Special Features" page from the main menu, and then tap the Right Arrow on your DVD remote. A "Rosebud" sled will appear—press Enter to be treated to a five-minute interview with actress Ruth Warrick (who plays Emily Kane in the film).

The second egg can be found in the "Production Notes" area. From here, visit the "In the Beginning" section and then choose "Still Galleries." By selecting the sleds, you will unlock hidden interviews with editor Robert Wise and film critic Roger Ebert.

Dante's Peak: Collector's Edition

Universal Pictures

Released 1997

Directed by Roger Donaldson

Starring Pierce Brosnan, Linda Hamilton

Dr. Harry Dalton (Pierce Brosnan) and Dante's Peak mayor Rachel Wando (Linda Hamilton) believe a dormant volcano is about to erupt, threatening the lives and homes of this peaceful town.

This "Collector's Edition" DVD features production design sketches, a look into the special effects of the film, trailers and posters, the shooting script, and of course, an Easter egg.

From the main menu, select "Bonus Materials" and then choose "Getting Close to the Show: The Making of Dante's Peak."

Once inside, select "Language Selection" and then "Spoken Language." Scroll down and press Enter over the words "Musical Score" and then over "Return to Movie" to watch this hour-long documentary with just the score.

Dark City

New Line Cinema

Released 1998

Directed by Alex Proyas

Starring Rufus Sewell, Kiefer Sutherland, Jennifer Connelly, Richard O'Brien, Ian Richardson, William Hurt

From the director of *The Crow* comes this twisted tale starring Rufus Sewell (as John Murdoch), who awakens in a hotel room to find himself wanted for a series of brutal murders.

Along with the widescreen and fullscreen versions of the film, a hidden game is also on the *Dark City* DVD.

From the main menu, select "Special Features" and then scroll down to the last entry, "To Shell Beach…" Once inside, read the rules for the game.

Need a spoiler? OK, here's how to solve it if you're stuck:

To find the bloody knife, go back to the "Special Features" menu, and select the first entry, "Cast & Crew." Now go to the "Kiefer Sutherland" biography, and once inside, press the Right Arrow two times; when a gray knife appears at the bottom of the screen, press Enter.

Now go back to the "Special Features" menu, and select "Neil Gaiman on Dark City." Once inside, press the Up Arrow and a blue business card will appear. Press Enter and the card will turn orange, leading you to more info.

Go back to the "Special Features" menu, and select the option "The Metropolis Comparison." Scroll down and choose "Original Weekly Variety Review," and scroll to the last page. When here, press the Up Arrow to highlight the postcard from Shell Beach and then press Enter.

Now go back to the "Cast & Crew" screen, and enter the biography of "Trevor Jones" on the second page. Now press "More" until you land on the tenth and final page of this biography, and press the Up Arrow to highlight the Shell Beach souvenir. Press Enter.

Go back to the "Cast & Crew" section and choose "William Hurt." Click "More" during his bio until the eighth and final page. Press the Up Arrow to highlight the clock and press Enter.

Finally, go back to the "Special Features" menu and choose "Set Designs" (second from the top). Once inside, click the word "More" until you land on the picture of the syringe. Press the Up Arrow and press Enter.

If you complete this Easter egg hunt in the correct sequence, you'll be treated to a very strange and psychedelic animated sequence.

The disc also contains two hidden video clips:

From the main menu, scroll down and choose "Special Features," and then press Enter to choose the first entry, "Cast & Crew." Now select "Kiefer Sutherland" and select the word "More" three times. An undocumented video clip from *Twin Peaks: Fire Walk with Me,* also starring Sutherland, will appear.

Now visit the "William Hurt" biography, and do the same thing—press "More" five times until you see a clickable *Lost in Space* clip featuring Hurt.

Detroit Rock City

New Line Entertainment

Released 1999

Directed by Adam Rifkin

Starring Edward Furlong, Giuseppe Andrews, James DeBello, Sam Huntington

P art road-trip flick, part coming of age story, this film takes place in 1978, when a high school rock band from Cleveland decides to travel to Detroit to pay homage to the greatest rock and roll band alive, KISS.

From the main menu of this DVD, scroll up until the small New Line logo is highlighted with the green stripe. Press Enter to go to an interactive credits screen. Press Enter over the first entry for "Angry Monkey," the folks responsible for the menu design on the DVD.

Select "More" to go to the second page. Now press Enter over the word "Facts" in the bottom-right corner of the screen. This will launch the silly yet entertaining video clip entitled "Facts," an Angry Monkey tale. Press Enter to go from one screen to the next.

Now head back to the credits section, and select "Three Legged Cat Productions," the team responsible for the commentaries and featurettes. Click "More" four times until the last page of "Special Thanks." Press Enter over the word "The Devil Roosevelt" for the picture of the band.

Lastly, go back and select "Tim Sullivan" at the bottom of the screen for a picture of him with the four KISS members in makeup.

Die Hard: Five Star Collection

20th Century Fox

Released 1988

Directed by John McTiernan

Starring Bruce Willis

Gutsy NYPD cop John McClane (Bruce Willis) flies to L.A. to spend Christmas with his estranged wife, but her holiday office party comes to an abrupt end when bond-stealing European terrorists lock down the high-rise building and take hostages as collateral.

Insert the second disc from this popular action flick, and instead of choosing from any of these bonus features, press the Up Arrow on the remote twice, and a red light will illuminate at the top middle of the helicopter landing pad.

Press Enter and before you know it, the high-rise building will blow up, followed by the words, "There Goes Fox Home Entertainment!"

On the same disc, select "From The Vault" from the main menu and then choose "Outtakes." Now select "The Vault." Once inside, press the Right Arrow twice, and a small white gun will appear on the screen. Press Enter and the gun will turn yellow before launching some outtakes from the film. (Note: There is music, but no dialogue.)

A less exciting egg is on the first disc. From the main menu, go to the "Language Selection" screen. Scroll down over the word "English" (under "Subtitles"), but do not press Enter just yet. Instead, press the Right Arrow, and a light will shine off the left side of Bruce Willis' face. Now press Enter to access a hidden DVD credits screen.

Die Hard 2: Die Harder

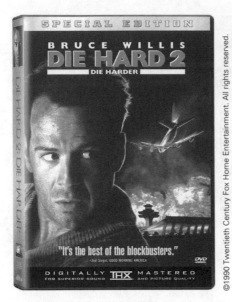

20th Century Fox

Released 1990

Directed by Renny Harlin

Starring Bruce Willis

Renegade terrorists seize a major international airport on Christmas Eve, holding thousands of holiday travelers hostage. Off-duty cop John McClane (Bruce Willis), who is experiencing somewhat of a déjà vu for this time of year, is determined to save the day (once again!).

This "Special Edition" double DVD (also found in the *Die Hard Trilogy* box set) features a number of making-of documentaries, featurettes, deleted scenes, storyboards, interviews, trailers, and TV spots.

There's a small egg, too.

Insert the second DVD ("Special Features"). From the main menu, scroll all the way to the bottom, and highlight the words "Visual Effects," but without pressing Enter just yet. Instead, tap the Right Arrow on the DVD remote, and the railing will turn white. Press Enter to read four full pages of DVD credits for the making of this collector's edition DVD set.

Die Hard with a Vengeance

20th Century Fox

Released 1995

Directed by John McTiernan

Starring Bruce Willis, Jeremy Irons, Samuel L. Jackson

Bruce Willis reprises his role as tough cop John McClane, who is now the target of the mysterious Simon (Jeremy Irons), a deadly terrorist hell-bent on blowing up the city of New York if he doesn't get what he wants. McClane is joined by an unwilling civilian, Zeus Carver (Samuel L. Jackson).

On the second DVD, select "Interview and Profile" from the main menu. Once inside, press the Left Arrow on the DVD remote, and the "Exit" sign in the subway will illuminate in white. Press Enter for an enjoyable collage of outtakes from the film.

"I'll get this right," smirks Willis, embarrassed, in one scene. In another, Jackson laughs and swears when Willis fouls up another line.

Now head back to the main menu, and highlight the words "Trailers and TV Spots," but do not press Enter. Instead, press the Right Arrow, and the subway post on the right side of the screen will glow white. Press Enter to read the credits for the DVD.

Dinosaur

Walt Disney Pictures

Released 2000

Directed by Eric Leighton, Ralph Zondag

Starring D.B. Sweeney, Alfre Woodard, Ossie Davis, Max Casella, Hayden Panettiere, Samuel E. Wright, Julianna Margulies, Peter Siragusa, Joan Plowright, Della Reese

Step back in time to an age where dinosaurs ruled the Earth. After a meteorite shower destroys his home, an orphaned dinosaur, Aladar, goes on an epic, eye-opening journey.

Disney's *Dinosaur* is a technical marvel that's perfect for kids and adults alike.

Along with the many features on this two-disc DVD set, is a handful of eggs.

Pop in the second disc and press the Left Arrow. The small sticky-note in the bottom-left corner of the screen will change to "DVD Credits." Press Enter to read four pages of who's responsible for this remarkable double-disc set.

Go back to the main menu, and select the first entry, "Development." Once inside, press the Right Arrow and the dinosaur's skull will illuminate in red. Press Enter to watch a lengthy black-and-white video showing Walt Disney chatting about the history of animating dinosaurs, highlighting the work of Windsor McCay, the famous newspaper cartoonist and his classic animation, "Gertie the Dinosaur."

Go back to the main menu, and select the second section, "Creating the Characters." Once again, tap the Right Arrow, and the dinosaur skull will turn red. Press Enter to watch a minute-and-a-half featurette of digital *Dinosaur* outtakes.

Now head back to the main menu, and scroll down to the third section, "The Production Process." Once inside, press the Right Arrow, and the dinosaur's skull will turn red. Press Enter to view a five-minute video featuring Walt Disney and three dinosaurs. This clip originally aired in 1964 to promote the World's Fair.

Lastly, return to the main menu, and choose the last section, "Publicity." Once inside, press the Right Arrow again; then press Enter and the dino skull will turn red. This will launch a 12-minute educational cartoon, "Recycle Rex," starring an environmentally friendly dinosaur!

Top 20 Worst Movies of All Time?

According to Web surfers who voted at the popular Internet Movie Database (www.imdb.com), the following are the top 20 worst movies of all time. Hey, where's *Howard the Duck*?

1. Backyard Dogs
2. Trigger Fast
3. Manos, the Hands of Fate
4. Girl in Gold Boots
5. Night Train to Mundo Fine
6. The Beast of Yucca Flats
7. Madmen of Mandoras
8. The Eye Creatures
9. Eegah
10. Uchu Kaisoku-sen
11. Mangler 2
12. Hobgoblins
13. Merlin's Shop of Mystical Wonders
14. Angelo, Fredo et Romeo
15. Zaat
16. Secret Agent Super Dragon
17. L'Uomo puma
18. The Wild World of Batwoman
19. Space Mutiny
20. The Skydivers

Dirty Dancing: Collector's Edition

Artisan

Released 1987

Directed by Emile Ardolino

Starring Jennifer Grey, Patrick Swayze, Jerry Orbach, Cynthia Rhodes

"Have the time of your life" with Frances "Baby" Houseman (Jennifer Grey), who, during a summer camp getaway with her family, falls in love with Johnny Castle (Patrick Swayze), the camp's dance teacher. At night, Castle, Houseman, and other dancers practice "Dirty Dancing."

From the main menu of this "Collector's Edition" DVD, select "Cast & Crew" and then choose the filmography/biography of "Patrick Swayze," "Jennifer Grey," and Dirty Dancing's director, "Emile Ardolino." (Note: Ardolino's bio is on the second page of this section.)

Use the Right Arrow to scroll through the pages of each bio (press Enter over the silhouette to advance to the next screen), and on the last page, the term "Q&A" will appear. Press the Right Arrow so that the "Q&A" turns blue. Now press Enter to read questions directed to that person.

What's hidden is that you can access video clips with their answers by pressing the Up Arrow and pressing Enter where the red ball appears.

Did You Know?

Actress Jennifer Grey was 27 years old when this movie was filmed, yet her character "Baby" Houseman was supposed to be many years younger.

Lead actor Patrick Swayze sang the hit song from this movie, "She's Like the Wind."

Donnie Darko

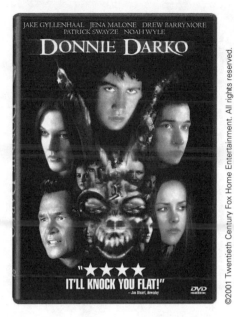

20th Century Fox

Released 2001

Directed by Richard Kelly

Starring Jake Gyllenhaal, Jena Malone, Drew Barrymore, Mary McDonnell, Katharine Ross, Patrick Swayze, Noah Wyle

In this underrated psychological thriller, Donnie Darko (Jake Gyllenhaal) is a troubled teen with strange delusions of the past, present, and future. A demonic, man-sized rabbit brings these disturbing, apocalyptic visions to Darko, and he must act on them despite the consequences.

From the main menu of this DVD, scroll to the right using the remote, and enter the "Special Features" submenu. Once inside, select the last entry on this page, "The Philosophy of Time Travel." Now click the Right Arrow to scroll through this book until you reach "Appendix A" (with the picture of the human body on it). Press the Up Arrow once, and a white circle will appear on the man's chest. Now press Enter to watch a deleted scene at a PTA meeting between characters Kitty Farmer (played by Beth Grant) and Karen Pomeroy (Drew Barrymore).

On the second "Appendix" screen—with the image of a man's skeleton facing toward the right—again press the Up Arrow, and the white arrow will turn black. Press Enter to watch the original theatrical trailer to the film.

There's one more egg on this DVD:

Go back out to the "Special Features" menu, and select the option "Cunning Visions." Once inside, scroll down four times until the words "Special Features" are highlighted. Press the Right Arrow and the small rectangular image will now have a white border. Press Enter to view 17 pages of a special web site gallery.

EDtv

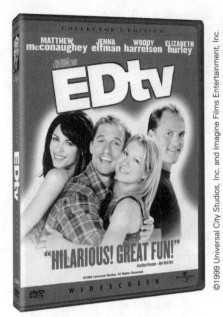

Universal Pictures

Released 1999

Directed by Ron Howard

Starring Matthew McConaughey, Jenna Elfman, Woody Harrelson, Elizabeth Hurley

E d Pekurny (Matthew McConaughey) is a regular guy who becomes the star of a hit reality TV show. His private life becomes a public soap opera spectacle as Ed falls in love with his brother's girlfriend (Jenna Elfman).

From the main menu, scroll up twice and select "Bonus Materials." Then tap the white arrow on the bottom of the screen to enter this section's second page.

Now select "Universal Showcase" to find undocumented trailers to other Universal Studios films including *Bowfinger* and *Mystery Men*.

There are two more trailers on this disc.

On the second page of "Bonus Materials," select "Cast and Filmmakers" and scroll to the second page to select director "Ron Howard." On the fourth page of his bio, you'll find a trailer for *Apollo 13*.

Lastly, there's a theatrical trailer for *EDtv* on the second page of "Bonus Materials."

Coolest-Looking DVD Boxes

Evil Dead: Book of the Dead Edition has a rubber/foam casing designed to resemble the book of the dead from the film.

Basic Instinct: Special Edition features a see-through plastic case that looks like a block of ice—and inside is a pen that resembles an ice pick.

The DVD case for *Total Recall: Special Edition* is a round red tin with bumps that resembles the planet Mars.

Terminator 2: Ultimate Edition, the *Rambo* box set, and *Highlander: Ultimate Edition* feature a cool metallic casing.

The Evil Dead: Book of the Dead Edition

Anchor Bay Entertainment

Released 1982

Directed by Sam Raimi

Starring Bruce Campbell, Ellen Sandweiss, Hal Delrich, Betsy Baker, Sarah York

This must-see classic horror film that launched Bruce "Ash" Campbell as the preeminent cult movie hero tells the tale of five teens who accidentally raise the dead while spending the night in a remote cabin. Don't you hate when that happens?

And as if this cool-looking DVD—with the soft rubber caseto resemble the actual "Book of the Dead" from the film—weren't enough to satiate fans, you can also uncover two hidden Easter eggs.

Select "Extras" from the main menu, and instead of picking from this list of options (which includes "Poster and Still Gallery" and "Commentaries"), tap the Left Arrow, and the transparent fish will illuminate on the right side of the screen. Now press Enter to watch a rare, minute-long "Special Make-Up Effects Test" video clip of a zombie's face decaying and bleeding. Lovely!

The second egg can be found once again on the "Extras" page. Choose "More" to be taken to the second batch of options. You may notice two transparent skulls on the screen. Press the Left Arrow, and the left skull one will turn blood red. Press Enter to watch a special behind-the-scenes video shot on Halloween 2001 when Anchor Bay Entertainment screened a new print of the Evil Dead to a capacity crowd at the American Cinematheque, Hollywood.

The Fast and the Furious

Universal Studios

Released 2001

Directed by Rob Cohen

Starring Paul Walker, Vin Diesel

Officer Brian O'Conner (Paul Walker) is an undercover cop who infiltrates a gang of L.A. street racers—posing as one of their own daredevil drivers—in order to solve a crime. But O'Connor falls in love with the sister of the ex-con gang leader, Domenic Toretto (Vin Diesel).

Like stunts? Then you'll definitely "flip" over the Easter eggs in this film.

From the main menu, select "Bonus Materials" and then scroll down to "Multiple Camera Angle Stunt Sequence" (second from the bottom). Press the Right Arrow, and a yellow steering wheel will appear on the right side of the screen. Press Enter to watch one of the last car stunts from the film—but from multiple angles. Great stuff.

Back in the "Bonus Materials" screen, select "Racer X: The Article That Inspired The Movie." When this article by Kenneth Li appears on the screen, press the Up Arrow and another yellow steering wheel will appear near the top. Press Enter to watch interviews with cast and crew members, interspersed with video footage from the film.

Also, let the credits roll at the end of the movie to be treated to a scene with Toretto (Diesel) cruising through Baja, Mexico.

Lastly, the DVD has a little-known demo of Activision's "Supercar Street Challenge" computer game embedded on the disc. It offers players two cars and two tracks to race on. It's a fun, arcade-like racing game, and a fitting addition to the fast-paced flick. Be sure to check the minimum system requirements to make sure your PC can run the game.

Fast Times at Ridgemont High

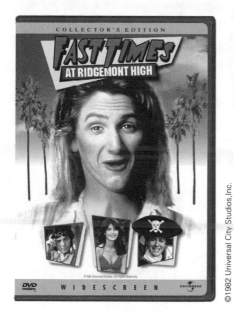

Universal Pictures

Released 1982

Directed by Amy Heckerling

Starring Sean Penn, Jennifer Jason Leigh, Judge Reinhold, Phoebe Cates, Brian Backer, Robert Romanus, Ray Walston

©1982 Universal City Studios, Inc.

This humorous tale of sex, drugs, and rock 'n' roll—written by Cameron Crowe—takes a peek into the misadventures of California teenagers in the early '80s. Who could forget Sean Penn's performance as the ultimate surfer dude (and stoner), Spicoli?

From the main menu, select "Bonus Materials" and you'll see a long list of options. Forget about them for now—instead, press the Up Arrow on the remote, and the small white footprints will turn red. Press Enter to be treated to classic quotes from the film including "All I need are some tasty waves, cool buds, and I'm fine."

Even better—click on any of these quotes to launch its corresponding video clip from the film.

More of these "classic quotes" pages can be found on the main menu for the DVD (in the upper-right corner of the screen) and in the "Languages" section (footprints on the bottom right).

Fear and Loathing in Las Vegas

© 1998 Universal Pictures Company.

Universal Studios

Released 1998

Directed by Terry Gilliam

Starring Johnny Depp, Benicio Del Toro

Based on the psychedelic book by H unter S. Thompson, this film follows journalist Raoul Duke (Johnny Depp) and his friend and lawyer, Dr. Gonzo (Benicio Del Toro), on a writing assignment in Las Vegas. Problem is, they've consumed almost every illegal narcotic imaginable, resulting in a hallucinatory adventure they won't soon forget.

Film fanatics who enjoy watching movie trailers will certainly have fun uncovering these gems—especially since they're well hidden.

From the main menu, select "Bonus Materials" and then select "Cast & Filmmakers." Scroll down to "Directed by Terry Gilliam" and press Enter. You can read his bio by scrolling through the text using the Right Arrow. If you notice, the second-to-last page features a trailer to *12 Monkeys* (1995), and the last page of the bio has a trailer to *Brazil* (1985), both directed by Gilliam.

Fiddler on the Roof: Special Edition

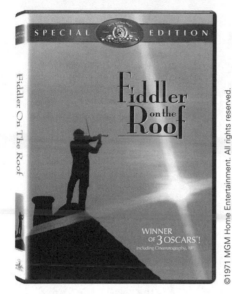

MGM

Released 1971

Directed by Norman Jewison

Starring Topol, Norma Crane, Leonard Frey, Molly Picon, Paul Mann

Based on the stories of Sholom Aleichem and the hit musical *Fiddler on the Roof,* this award- winning film takes place in early 20th century Russia as a Jewish peasant, Tevye (Topol), attempts to preserve tradition while marrying off his three daughters and coping with a changing political climate.

Pop in the "Special Features" side of the disc, and from the main menu, highlight the words "The Stories of Sholom Aleichem," but don't press Enter just yet. Instead, tap the Right Arrow on the DVD remote, and a small yellow silhouette of a fiddler sitting on a roof will appear. Press Enter and enjoy this short video of director Norman Jewison telling a story about a rich merchant and a beggar.

Allegedly, this story was heard during the original stage play of *Fiddler on the Roof,* but failed to make it into the film.

Field of Dreams: Collector's Edition

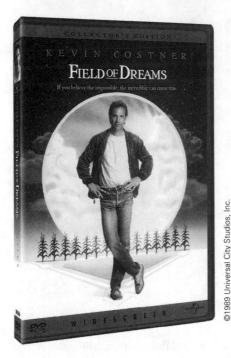

©1989 Universal City Studios, Inc.

Universal Studios

Released 1989

Directed by Phil Alden Robinson

Starring Kevin Costner, Amy Madigan, Ray Liotta, James Earl Jones, Burt Lancaster

"If you build it, he will come" is the classic line from this magical baseball movie.

Cash-strapped Iowa farmer Ray Kinsella (Kevin Costner) and his supportive wife Annie (Amy Madigan) decide to build a baseball diamond on their land, which is then visited by the ghosts of Shoeless Joe Jackson and several other Chicago White Sox players.

From the main menu, select "Bonus Materials" and the screen will offer five options. Select the first header ("The Field of Dreams Scrapbook"). Next, choose "Language Selection," and then "Spoken Language," and you'll see an option for "Musical Score."

Press Enter to watch the "Field of Dreams Scrapbook" documentary, but with only the soothing soundtrack in 5.1 surround sound.

Also, while it's not quite an egg, listen carefully on the "Bonus Materials" page, and you'll hear some dialogue from the film where Kevin Costner is told by a ghost to "Ease his pain."

Fight Club

20th Century Fox

Released 1999

Directed by David Fincher

Starring Brad Pitt, Edward Norton, Helena Bonham Carter

Two unlikely associates begin an underground therapy group called the "Fight Club," and the concept catches on across America. A surprise twist near the end of the film had audiences buzzing, winning Brad Pitt and Edward Norton a nomination for "Best Action Team" at the 2000 Blockbuster Entertainment Awards.

Insert the second "Supplemental" disc, and from the main menu, scroll across the bottom of the screen (using the Right Arrow), to select the "Advertising" tab. Once inside this new screen, press the Down Arrow a few times until a green smiley face appears in the lower-left corner of the screen. Now press Enter to view some of the official *Fight Club* merchandise such as soap bars, T-shirts, a golf shirt, backpack, clock, and more.

Be sure to read the entertaining descriptions for each of these products and how each ties into the film.

Another small egg can be found on the first disc. From the main menu, scroll across the bottom of the screen, and stop over the words "Special." Press the Up Arrow on the DVD remote, and another green smiley face will appear on the screen. Press Enter to view the production credits for this two-disc DVD set.

Did You Know?

Actors Brad Pitt and Edward Norton were intoxicated during the filming of the scene where they "play" drunk while practicing their golf swing. Allegedly, the balls were hitting the side of the catering truck!

A Fish Called Wanda

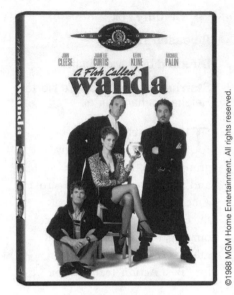

MGM

Released 1988

Directed by Charles Crichton

Starring John Cleese, Jamie Lee Curtis, Kevin Kline, Michael Palin

In this hilarious romantic comedy about thievery, trickery, and titillation, four unlikely jewelry store robbers band together to steal precious diamonds in London. But Wanda (Jamie Lee Curtis) and her boyfriend Otto (Kevin Kline) want the loot for themselves, so they call the cops on the ringleader, George (Tom Georgeson), who hides the diamonds in an unlikely place before he's arrested.

From this DVD's main menu, use the remote to navigate over to the treasure chest floating above the word "Languages." The lid of the chest will turn orange—press Enter and watch as the words and music fade, leaving nothing but this soothing aquarium screensaver!

To return to normal, press Enter again.

FM

Anchor Bay Entertainment

Released 1978

Directed by John A. Alonzo

Starring Michael Brandon, Eileen Brennan, Alex Karras, Cleavon Little, Martin Mull, Cassie Yates

Los Angeles' most popular DJ, Jeff Dugan (Michael Brandon), and the wacky staff at QSKY will do anything to save the radio station from its money-hungry corporate officers who want to play more commercials and less rock 'n' roll.

The film includes performances by Tom Petty, REO Speedwagon, Jimmy Buffet, and Linda Ronstadt.

The egg on this DVD is quite easy to find—in fact, you don't have to do anything.

While almost all DVDs have a short, looped audio track that plays during the main menu, *FM* has an entire song if you let it play. Pop in the disc and from the main menu, turn up the volume and enjoy the entire "Tumbling Dice," performed by Rondstadt.

For the Love of the Game

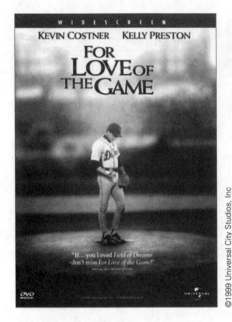

Universal Studios

Released 1999

Directed by Sam Raimi

Starring Kevin Costner, Kelly Preston

Aging pitcher Billy Chapel (Kevin Costner) faces the end of his career just as his on-again off-again girlfriend Jane Aubrey (Kelly Preston) announces she's leaving him for a job in England. Much of the film takes place during Chapel's last game of the season, and through a series of flashbacks chronicling the ups and downs of his relationship with Aubrey.

While it's not quite an Easter egg since it's easily found on the disc, a trivia game on this DVD yields a special surprise for those who successfully answer all the questions.

From the main menu, scroll down and select the "On the Mound" baseball trivia game. If you get all 12 answers correct before you get three strikes, you'll hit a "Grand Slam." What does this mean? Sit back and enjoy a special 15-minute black-and-white short movie entitled "Slide, Babe, Slide," a 1931 film about Babe Ruth.

Fried Green Tomatoes: Collector's Edition

©1991 Fried Green Tomatoes Productions

Universal Studios

Released 1991

Directed by Jon Avnet

Starring Kathy Bates, Jessica Tandy, Mary Stuart Masterson, Mary-Louise Parker

This heartwarming "chick flick" takes place in a small Georgia town, Whistle Stop, where unhappily married Evelyn Couch (Kathy Bates) visits a nursing home and listens to an inspiring story spun by the elder Ninny Threadgoode (Jessica Tandy).

Common in many Universal DVD movies is a hidden musical score, but this one can be a little tricky to find. Here's how to do it:

From the main menu, select "Bonus Materials" and then select the documentary, "Moments of Discovery: The Making of Fried Green Tomatoes." Now, instead of selecting "Play," scroll down and select "Language." On the left of the screen, you'll see "Musical Score." Tap the Left Arrow on the remote, and the words "Musical Score" will be highlighted with red borders. Press Enter to watch the documentary—but with only the classical music score playing in the background.

Friends: The Complete First Season

Warner Bros.

TV Series

Began 1994

Starring Jennifer Aniston, Courteney Cox, Lisa Kudrow, Matt LeBlanc, Matthew Perry, David Schwimmer

This complete season-one box set of *Friends*—one of the most successful TV sitcoms in history— features four DVDs packed with more than 20 episodes, special features, and an Easter egg, too.

Insert the fourth disc from this set, and select "Special Features" from the main menu. Now press Enter to select the first of these features, "Friends of Friends." This page is a guestbook of celebrities—such as Jay Leno, Helen Hunt, and George Clooney—who have appeared on the show. Selecting any of these will launch a video clip with their appearances.

This isn't the egg, of course, but if you press the Left Arrow from this "Friends of Friends" screen, you'll notice that the steaming coffee cup in the upper-left corner of the screen will now have a blue circle around it. Press Enter to watch a casting call take place during a show (where Joey [Matt LeBlanc] was trying out for a part); little does the audience know that the three "casting directors" are none other than *Friends*' executive producers Kevin Bright, Martha Kauffman, and David Crane.

From Hell

20ᵗʰ Century Fox

Released 2001

Directed by Albert Hughes, Allen Hughes

Starring Johnny Depp, Heather Graham

From Hell embarks on a chilling journey of bloodlust, back when Jack the Ripper terrorized the streets of London at the turn of the 20ᵗʰ century. Johnny Depp plays a drug-addicted clairvoyant detective, Fred Abberline, who with a homeless prostitute, Mary Kelly (Heather Graham), is determined to catch Jack the Ripper in the act.

From the main menu of the second DVD, scroll down and highlight the words "Absinthe Makes The Heart Grow Fonder," but don't press Enter. Instead, press the Down Arrow and then the Right Arrow, and the scalpel in the travel kit will illuminate in white. Press Enter to watch a 40-minute UK film, *Jack The Ripper: The Final Solution,* based on Stephen Knight's classic book.

Now switch discs and pop in the first DVD.

From the main menu, select "Language Selection" and then scroll down to the bottom of the screen until the words "Main Menu" are highlighted. Instead of pressing Enter, press the Right Arrow on the DVD remote, and the eye will open. Now press Enter to view the DVD credits.

Go back to the main menu and select "Special Features." Press the number 5 on the remote, and a yellow silhouette of Jack the Ripper will appear, followed by a THX demonstration.

Gladiator

TM & ©2000 DreamWorks L.L.C. and Universal Pictures, reprinted with permission by DreamWorks L.L.C. and Universal Pictures.

DreamWorks Pictures

Released 2000

Directed by Ridley Scott

Starring Russell Crowe

In this Academy Award–winning feature film, Roman general Maximus (Russell Crowe) seeks revenge for the murder of his family. Now a slave, his only way to get back to Rome to face his nemesis—the corrupt Emperor Commodus (Joaquin Phoenix)—is to become a gladiator.

There are two good Easter eggs on this critically acclaimed action epic.

Insert the second disc and scroll down to select the word "More." Now visit the "Trailers and TV Spots" area. Ignore all of these options, and press the Left Arrow on the remote; the amulet around the neck of Emperor Marcus Aurelius (Richard Harris) will turn red. Press Enter and enjoy a hilarious *Chicken Run* trailer modeled after the dramatic *Gladiator* theme ("An egg that became a chicken, a chicken that became a leader!" and so forth). Great fun.

Another egg can be found on this second disc by going to "Original Storyboards." Click on the "More" tab and choose "Rhino Fight." Press the Up Arrow and the rhino in the middle of the screen will turn gray. Press Enter to read about a deleted scene featuring a rhinoceros, view the related script and storyboard sequence, and even watch test footage of a digitally created rhino.

The Godfather—DVD Collection

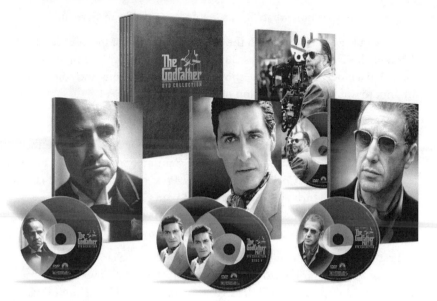

Paramount Pictures

Released 1972 (The Godfather), 1974 (The Godfather: Part II), 1990 (The Godfather: Part III)

Directed by Francis Ford Coppola

Starring Marlon Brando, Al Pacino, Diane Keaton, Robert De Niro, Richard S. Castellano, Robert Duvall, James Caan, John Cazale, Andy Garcia

This five-disc trilogy chronicles the infamous lives of the Corleone mob family through multiple generations.

There are a few good eggs buried deep inside this collection, and all of them can be found on the fourth disc, "Bonus Materials."

From the main menu, select the "SetUp" section, and then tap the Right Arrow on the DVD remote. A globe will appear on the screen. Press Enter and enjoy this humorous collage of famous *Godfather* scenes—but in multiple languages as seen throughout the world.

Ever wanted to know what "Ba-da-boom" sounds like in German?

A second egg can be found in the "Galleries" section of the disc. Scroll down to "DVD Credits" and press Enter. Now click "Next" four times to be treated to a hidden clip from the show *The Sopranos* as Tony and company attempt to watch a bootleg version of *The Godfather* on DVD!

There's more…

From the main menu, select the option "The Family Tree." Now use the DVD remote to navigate around and select "Santino ('Sonny')." Press Enter again to launch Sonny Corleone's biography. Press the Left Arrow and James Caan's picture will turn white. Press Enter to read Caan's biography. Press the Left Arrow again, and this new picture of him will also turn white. Press Enter—now you can watch his screen tests as Sonny Corleone.

Lastly, from the main menu, select the word "Filmmakers" and once inside, enter the "Mario Puzo" biography. Press the Left Arrow twice, and a large, green dollar sign will fill the screen. Press Enter to view a humorous conversation between Francis Ford Coppola and Mario Puzo as they play pool. Coppola asks Puzo why he wrote the book *The Godfather*. His answer? "To make money!"

Hackers

MGM

Released 1995

Directed by Iain Softley

Starring Jonny Lee Miller, Angelina Jolie, Fisher Stevens, Lorraine Bracco

In this film set during the dawn of the Information Age, a young computer genius and his pals pull off a near-impossible task of hacking into a highly secured computer at the Ellington Mineral Corporation. But in doing so, they stumble upon a high-tech embezzling scheme masked by a computer virus.

Hackers was also the film to put Angelina Jolie on the map.

Looking to hack into the DVD to find its egg? No need—here's how to locate it:

From the main menu, press the Left Arrow on the remote, and the logo for *Hackers* will illuminate in beige.

Press Enter on the remote, and this will take you to a screen where you're asked to input the proper password from the list of options: Sex, Secret, Love, or God.

Use the remote to navigate over the word "God," press Enter, and the words "Access Granted" will flash on the screen. Following this will be a short computer-generated sequence of soaring through the insides of a computer.

Hannibal

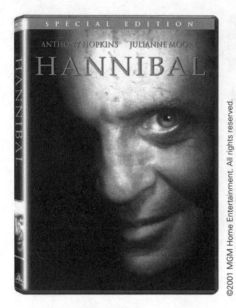

MGM

Released 2001

Directed by Ridley Scott

Starring Anthony Hopkins, Julianne Moore

D r. Hannibal Lecter (Anthony Hopkins) is back in this creepy sequel to *Silence of the Lambs.* The intelligent, perverse, and manipulative killer lures FBI agent Clarice Starling (Julianne Moore) into a deadly game of survival and suspense.

Insert the "Special Features" DVD (disc 2) and from the main menu, select the first option: "Breaking the Silence, The Making of Hannibal."

Now scroll down and place the cursor over the "Music" option, but don't press Enter. Instead, press the Left Arrow on the DVD remote, and the two little up arrows will change to blue. Now press Enter to watch a few minutes of Clarice's "Flashframes," the brief bursts of film exposed from the time a director yells "Cut!" to the moment the camera is turned off.

Another point of interest: *Hannibal* music editor Mark Streitenfeld performed, wrote, and produced an original song entitled "Clarice" specifically for this unusual montage.

Harry Potter and the Sorcerer's Stone

Warner Bros.

Released 2001

Directed by Chris Columbus

Starring Daniel Radcliffe, Rupert Grint, Emma Watson

One of the most successful contemporary book series for kids (aged 7 to 77) makes its way onto the silver screen. *Harry Potter and the Sorcerer's Stone* tells the tale of young Harry Potter as he attends the Hogwarts School of Witchcraft and Wizardry.

From the main menu, press the Right Arrow on the DVD remote, and the owl will have some magic sparkles around it. Press Enter to read that you've been accepted at Hogwarts School of Witchcraft and Wizardry. You'll also be instructed to insert disc 2.

From the main menu of the second disc, choose "Diagon Alley" and you'll be told to choose the bricks in the correct sequence in order to enter the alley. The solution is to work counterclockwise. On the DVD remote, press the Left Arrow, Up Arrow, Up Arrow again, and then press Enter. Next press the Up Arrow and then Enter. Now it's Up Arrow and then Enter again. Now tap the Right Arrow, Down Arrow, Down Arrow again, and Enter. Lastly, it's Down Arrow and then Enter. This will give you access. Don't worry—if you mess up, the bricks will move and you'll be let in soon enough.

Now you'll be inside the alleyway (as in the film!). Before you purchase a wand, you'll need money, so access the "Gringotts" bank. When you navigate to the Gringotts sign, press the Down Arrow, and the key will be highlighted. Now press Enter to get inside the bank.

Once inside, press the Down Arrow and the jellybeans will be highlighted. Press Enter for a close-up of "Every Flavour Beans." Click around the screen with the DVD remote to read about a few of the flavors offered.

OK, down to business:

While at the bank, tap the Right Arrow and then Enter to open your vault. Take a look at that stash of gold and silver! Listen to the instructions for a clue on what to do next. Exit to the alley and then enter "Ollivanders" wand store. It doesn't matter which wand you choose by navigating around the shelves with the DVD remote—after a few wrong (and explosive!) picks, the right one will be handed to you.

Once you have your wand, it's time for class. Head back to the main menu, and select "Classrooms" from the middle of the screen. Here, select "Potions" and once inside this new screen, press the Right Arrow to highlight the mortar and pestle. Press Enter. Now choose the right ingredients to make each of the three potions and then mix them. "But do be careful," warns your narrator.

First, choose to create a sleeping potion. Do this by selecting "Wormwood" and "Asphodel" (by pressing Enter over both vials). Now you're asked what another name is for "Aconite." The correct answer is "Monkshood" and "Wolfsbane," so select these from the vials by pressing Enter on both. Next, you're asked what you need to cure a boil! The answer, of course, is "Porcupine Quills" and "Snake Fangs." Press Enter on both of these ingredients to pass this stage of the game.

Now you must look for a key (among many flying keys). The correct one can be chosen by pressing the following on the DVD remote: Right Arrow, Up Arrow, Up Arrow again, Right Arrow, and then Enter. It'll be the small key in the back.

If you've kept up this far, good for you! But your work is still not done yet. Take a look at this screen and you must now select from one of the seven bottles available here – within 60 seconds. The answer is the yellow round one in the middle. Scroll over to it and press Enter.

And here's the payoff—you'll be taken to the magic mirror and handed the sorcerer's stone. Press the Up Arrow and then Enter to take it. Congratulations—you will be transported through the mirror to a secret screen with seven fantastic bonus videos, including many deleted scenes from the film.

(Note: There are other ways to access this Sorcerer's Stone, which will unlock the extra goodies. The above scenario is but one! Enjoy trying to find other ways to access this hidden material.)

Did You Know?

There are some fun continuity errors to try and catch in the film. Here are a couple of them:

On the train to Hogwarts, Ron Weasley's hair is parted in different places throughout the ride. You'll see it go from a part in the middle to no part at all once he asks Harry about his scar!

After arriving at Hogwarts, Harry takes a seat opposite Hermione Granger, but in the following cut (when the feast begins), he's right beside her! Now that's magic!

Highlander 4: Endgame

Dimension Films

Released 2000

Directed by Douglas Aarniokoski

Starring Adrian Paul, Christopher Lambert

To combat a ruthless and relentless band of immortals, Connor Macleod (Christopher Lambert) and his brother Duncan (Adrian Paul) team up to battle the forces of darkness. Remember, in the end, there can be only one!

From the main menu of the first disc, press the Left Arrow, and a yellow insignia will appear. Press Enter and the screen will explain that this is just one of six "Watcher Files" planted on this disc. You'll need to find the other five to beat Jacob Kell in the "There can be only one" trivia game on this disc.

The first hint, for example, is that Connor Macleod was an early pioneer in the orange juice business, but he later found the antique business better suited to his lifestyle.

Some of these Watcher Files contain video clips, too.

The second and third Watcher symbols can be found in the "Bonus Materials" menu by pressing the Left Arrow in the "Feature Audio Commentary" section, and in the "Deleted Scenes" section on the second page of "Bonus Materials."

The last three symbols are in the "Captions" section, the "Sneak Peeks" section, and the "DVD-ROM" section—all from the main menu. For each of these three symbols, press the Left Arrow and then press Enter.

How High

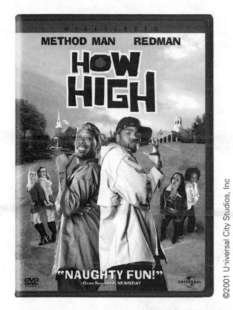

Universal Pictures

Released 2001

Directed by Jesse Dylan

Starring Method Man and Redman

Consider this movie as hip-hop meets Cheech & Chong. Two unlikely Harvard students (played by rappers Method Man and Redman) shake things up a little at the Ivy League school with their penchant for partying.

There's a little Easter egg hunt to try on the DVD, with some help from Method Man and Redman.

From the main menu, enter the "Bonus Materials" page, and scroll down to highlight the words "Hide the Stash." Press the Right Arrow. A red cigarette lighter will appear on the chalkboard. Press Enter to watch a humorous clip of "Pimpology 101."

Go to the second page of "Bonus Materials." Highlight the words "Music Videos," and then press the Left Arrow, and the number 420 will turn red at the top of the screen. Press Enter.

"Sorry bro," they'll tell you. This isn't it.

Now, while still on the second page of "Bonus Materials," scroll down and highlight the words "Universal Showcase." Now press the Right Arrow, and the number 420 will turn red at the bottom of the screen. Press Enter.

"That's not it—you're too cold!"

Click "More" to be taken to the third and final page of "Bonus Materials," scroll down to highlight the arrow beside the word "Back," and then press the Up Arrow. The number *420* will turn red. Press Enter.

"Damn, use your brain!" they yell.

Now scroll down to highlight the words "DVD Newsletter" and press the Right Arrow; the number *420* will turn red between the two girls on the right. Press Enter.

"Whoa! You finally found it, huh? It only took you about, what, 48 days?"

How to Clean Your DVDs

It's happened to all of us—you're trying to watch a DVD, but the disc is "stuttering" worse than Ken in *A Fish Called Wanda*. What to do? You could purchase one of those cleaning kits at your local retailer, or you can try the cheaper home remedy—and it works. Take a cotton cloth or any smooth towel (note: do not use tissues), and find some rubbing alcohol (even cheap perfume will do). Hold the DVD by its outer rim, spray a *bit* of the liquid onto the underside of the disc (the part the laser reads), and gently wipe in clockwise circles from the inside out. Be sure to wait until it dries before putting it back into the player. Chances are, you've removed most or all of the dirt from the grooves.

Independence Day

20th Century Fox

Released 1996

Directed by Roland Emmerich

Starring Will Smith, Bill Pullman, Jeff Goldblum

In one of the biggest sci-fi flicks in Hollywood history, the fate of the human race is at stake as Earth is invaded by war-hungry aliens in huge spaceships. A band of survivors vows to fight back, including Capt. Steven "Eagle" Hiller (Will Smith), U.S. President Thomas J. Whitmore (Bill Pullman), and ex-scientist David Levinson (Jeff Goldblum).

The two-disc "Five Star Collection" DVD features two versions of the film and a slew of bonus materials.

Pop in the second DVD, and from the main menu, select "Data Console" in the bottom-right corner of the screen. Once inside, highlight the words "Main Menu," but don't press Enter—tap the Right Arrow instead, and a little red light will appear on the personal computer. Press Enter and the disc will be inserted into the PC. "Systems Activated—Access 7-4-Enter" will flash on the screen. Also notice that the spaceship is floating in the background.

"Access 7-4-Enter" is a clue on what to do next.

Click on "Main Menu" and you'll see the ship is hovering. You only have seven seconds to punch in the password, which is "7," "4," and then Enter. Having done this, you'll now be inside the spacecraft. On some DVD players, you'll need to press the "10+" button seven times, followed by the "4," and then Enter. Experiment to get it right—because the payoff is worth it. (Remember, Independence Day is July 4th—hence the "7" and "4.")

This new menu screen inside the ship offers a handful of hidden features including isolated audio tracks, explosion scenes from the movie, fake news broadcasts created for the film, extended sequences, DVD credits, and more.

Jacob's Ladder: Special Edition

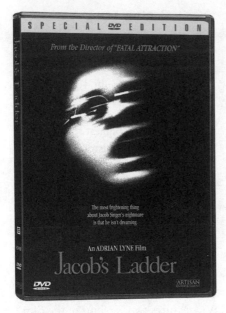

Artisan

Released 1990

Directed by Adrian Lyne

Starring Tim Robbins

This psychological horror follows the disillusion of a dying Vietnam vet, Jacob Singer (played by Tim Robbins). Singer and the audience are taken on a twisted and terrifying journey where it becomes difficult to tell what's real.

Though not specified on the DVD box, a handful of extras are stored on the *Jacob's Ladder* "Special Edition" DVD. They include numerous deleted scenes, deleted scenes with commentary, full-length audio commentary for the entire film, a promotional TV spot, and a 26-minute "making-of" documentary entitled "Building Jacob's Ladder."

Although these features are not exactly hidden, they are indeed unadvertised and undocumented features worth mentioning (and viewing!).

Jay and Silent Bob Strike Back

Dimension Films/Buena Vista Pictures

Released 2000

Directed by Kevin Smith

Starring Ben Affleck, Eliza Dushku, Shannon Elizabeth, Will Ferrell, Ali Larter, Jason Lee, Jason Mewes, Kevin Smith, Chris Rock

Jay (Jason Mewes) and Silent Bob (Kevin Smith), two buds from past Kevin Smith films such as *Clerks, Mallrats, Chasing Amy,* and *Dogma,* head out on a cross-country road trip from New Jersey to Hollywood. It seems a major motion picture is being based on their likeness, and they want to get the cash they deserve.

If you want to see Mewes' privates (no kidding), then you may want to unlock this DVD Easter egg. But you've been forewarned...

Insert the second disc and then click "More" to go to the second page of special features. Now select "Cast and Crew Filmographies," and then choose "Jason Mewes—Jay." Once inside, press the Up Arrow on the DVD remote until the word "Balls" appears at the top of the screen in red.

Now press Enter to see Mewes pull down his pants (facing away from the camera), exposing his, er, manhood. (Warning: nudity.)

Joy Ride

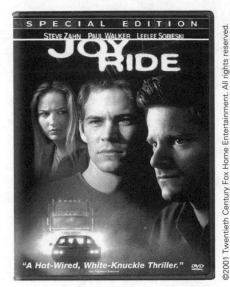

20th Century Fox

Released 2001

Directed by John Dahl

Starring Paul Walker, Steve Zahn, Leelee Sobieski

On this nail-biting thrill-ride, brothers Lewis and Fuller Thomas (Paul Walker and Steve Zahn) play a prank on a lonely truck driver who doesn't take the joke too well. Their cross-country drive with Lewis' college friend Venna Wilcox (Leelee Sobieski) becomes a deadly flight for their lives from the vengeful trucker who won't give up the chase until the boys have been taught a lesson.

From the disc's main menu, select the "Extra Features" menu at the bottom of the screen, and then select "Deleted Scene and Alternate Endings."

Now press the Up Arrow, and the car's taillights will turn red. Press Enter to read the DVD production credits.

And while they're not an egg, be sure to view the four alternate endings to this suspenseful film. What a treat!

Jurassic Park III: Collector's Edition

Universal Pictures

Released 2001

Directed by Joe Johnston

Starring Sam Neill, William H. Macy, Téa Leoni

©2001 Universal City Studios, Inc.

Renowned paleontologist Dr. Alan Grant (Sam Neill) agrees to accompany wealthy adventurer Paul Kirby (William H. Macy) and his wife, Amanda (Téa Leoni), on an aerial tour of Isla Sorna, InGen's former breeding ground for dinosaurs. The plane crashes onto the island, and the gang must (once again) outrun and outsmart the prehistoric beasts.

While not quite a dinosaur-sized Easter egg, there's an interesting undocumented extra planted on this "Collector's Edition" DVD.

From the main menu, scroll down to the second option, and select "Bonus Materials." Now click to the second page and select "Jurassic Park III Archives." The "Poster Gallery" inside, once selected, will display a slide show of 20 or so *Jurassic Park III* posters for the film.

These "Jurassic Park III Archives" also provide a montage of photos from the film that scroll by with the movie's theme music playing in the background.

Kiss of the Dragon

20th Century Fox

Released 2001

Directed by Chris Nahon

Starring Jet Li, Bridget Fonda

Wrapped up in a deadly conspiracy and falsely accused of murder, China's top intelligence agent Liu Jian (Jet Li) is on the run in Paris with the help of a seductive call girl, Jessica (Bridget Fonda), whose daughter is locked away in an orphanage.

The DVD of this martial arts thriller features a handful of extras including commentaries, featurettes, trailers, and of course, an Easter egg.

From the main menu, scroll across to the right, and press Enter over the "Special Features" tab. Once inside, click down to "Police Gymnasium Fight: Martial Arts Demo" and press Enter. Now scroll down and highlight the words "Demo Two," but instead of pressing Enter, press the Right Arrow on the DVD remote, and a silver dragon will appear on Jet Li's black shirt.

Press Enter to view an alternate, extended trailer for *Kiss of the Dragon*.

The Lawnmower Man

New Line Cinema

Released 1992

Directed by Brett Leonard

Starring Jeff Fahey, Pierce Brosnan, Jenny Wright

A brilliant scientist, Dr. Lawrence Angelo (Pierce Brosnan), uses an experimental virtual-reality treatment on the simple lawnmower man, Jobe Smith (Jeff Fahey). But unbeknownst to Dr. Angelo, his company alters the software and switches the enhancement drugs in the hopes of engineering a relentless killing machine.

The instant cult classic features a hidden puzzle game.

Insert the "Movie" side of the disc, and then select "Special Features" from the main menu. Scroll down to "The Cast" and instead of pressing Enter, press the Left Arrow. You'll see eight lime-green hexagons lit up to the left of the screen. Press Enter.

Enjoy this puzzle memory game comprised of yellow, blue, and red hexagons. Selecting the right piece in the correct order will flash "Access Granted" on the screen; selecting the wrong pieces will flash "Access Denied."

Complete the entire sequence and you'll see the words "You've Beaten the Lawnmower Man!" along with a humorous animated graphic.

Liar Liar: Collector's Edition

Universal Studios

Released 1997

Directed by Tom Shadyac

Starring Jim Carrey, Jennifer Tilly, Swoosie Kurtz, Amanda Donohoe

A lawyer who isn't allowed to lie? This is grounds for a good comedy. Attorney Fletcher Reede (Jim Carrey) must tell the truth in and out of the courtroom for an entire day, thanks to his son's magical birthday wish.

The DVD "Collector's Edition" of *Liar Liar* contains a few hidden trailers to other Universal movies.

From the main menu, scroll up above the word "Play," and press Enter over "Bonus Materials." On the second page of these materials, select "Cast and Filmmakers" and scroll all the way to the bottom to select "Directed by Tom Shadyac." (An easier way is to press the Up Arrow once!) Press the Right Arrow three times, and you'll find two video trailers to other Shadyac films, including the 1996 remake of *The Nutty Professor* and *Patch Adams* (1998).

The Limey

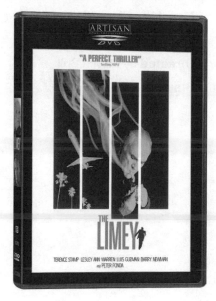

Artisan Entertainment

Released 1999

Directed by Steven Soderbergh

Starring Terence Stamp, Lesley Ann Warren, Luis Guzman, Barry Newman, Peter Fonda

Relentless British ex-con Wilson (Terence Stamp) travels to Los Angeles to investigate his daughter's so-called "accidental" death. Wilson's prime suspect is the wealthy music promoter Terry Valentine (Peter Fonda), who had had an affair with Wilson's daughter.

Let's face it—chances are you haven't read many of those dry and boring crew or cast biographies found on most of today's DVDs, right? Well, the creators of the DVD for *The Limey* thought they'd spice up the section for you.

From the disc's main menu, select "Special Features" and then choose the "Cast & Crew" option. Once inside, choose the biography of producer Scott Kramer—but don't expect to read his real bio. Instead, a humorous, fictitious one is posted.

For example, one line says, "In 1978, when he was eighteen, Kramer's family traded him to a religious group of tool salesmen for a wrench and a can of hairspray." This faux bio is three pages long.

Little NIcky

New Line Cinema

Released 2000

Directed by Steven Brill

Starring Adam Sandler

It's not easy being the son of the devil. Little Nicky (Adam Sandler) must visit Earth for the first time to find and bring back his two rebellious brothers, who have escaped the underworld and are raising hell in New York City. Can this lovable misfit really save humanity?

There are a couple of well-hidden Easter eggs on this "New Line Platinum Series" disc.

From the main menu, select the "Special Features" sign. You'll now have three possible paths—choose the middle one ("Central Park"), and an image of Little Nicky on a park bench will appear. Rather than selecting from the list of features to the right, move down to the word "Documentaries," and then press the Left Arrow. Now a yellow halo will appear over Little Nicky's head. Press Enter and enjoy an extensive trailer to New Line's fantasy film *The Lord of the Rings.*

Now go back to the "Special Features" menu, and do the same thing again—press the Left Arrow when the word "Documentaries" is highlighted so that a yellow halo appears over Sandler's head. Instead of pressing Enter, press the Left Arrow, then the Down Arrow, and then the Right Arrow, and a special interactive version of the movie will begin. Press the right Skip button, and some information will be available on the bottom of the screen.

You can now press Enter at various points in the film (or press the right Skip button often) to read biographies, see hidden interviews, watch deleted scenes and music videos, and much more.

Highlights include alternate Rodney Dangerfield lines, bloopers "from hell," veteran rock stars discussing the origins of heavy metal and why it was an important part of this film, a disturbing dart scene, and extra Jon Lovitz material.

Lastly, go back to the main menu of the DVD, and scroll down to highlight the words "Scene Selection." Now press the Right Arrow, and the Infinifilm logo will turn white. Press Enter to read the DVD credits for this disc.

Logan's Run

Warner Bros.

Released 1976

Directed by Michael Anderson

Starring Michael York, Richard Jordan, Jenny Agutter, Roscoe Lee Browne, Farrah Fawcett, Michael Anderson Jr., Peter Ustinov

In this sci-fi adventure, citizens of a confined, futuristic world are not permitted to live past the age of 30. Logan 5 (Michael York) is a policing "Sandman," responsible for chasing down and apprehending "Runners"— those who try to escape. But with the help of his love interest, Jessica 6 (Jenny Agutter), Logan discovers the truth about this society and decides to escape and seek out a place known as "Sanctuary," where people are free.

Fans of this classic film will enjoy the egg planted on the disc.

From the DVD's main menu, press the Right Arrow on the DVD, and the crystal in the hand will turn purple. Now press Enter to read the *Logan's Run* Life Clock description and images. For example, a white crystal means the bearer is 8 years of age or younger. Yellow is for ages 9 through 15; green means ages 16 to 23; and red is for ages 24 to Lastday (that is, 30 years old).

Watch the movie again and take note!

Lost in Space

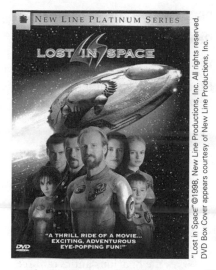

New Line Cinema

Released 1998

Directed by Stephen Hopkins

Starring William Hurt, Gary Oldman, Mimi Rogers, Heather Graham

In this remake of the popular '60s TV series, the Robinson family sets off into space to begin colonizing the planet Alpha Prime, when a stowaway sabotages the mission, thus causing the ship to become "lost in space."

There are a couple of hidden goodies buried on this DVD.

The first is a secret trivia game—pop the disc into the player, and from the main menu, select "Features" and then "Your Mission." Players are then asked to take control of the Jupiter 2 ship and lead the Robinson family to Alpha Prime. To achieve this, enter the correct info into the ship's onboard computer to activate the hyperdrive. The information to enter—which includes trivia tidbits on the movie, the cast, and the original show—can be found elsewhere on the disc.

Completing the entire game correctly will unlock a very funny joke reel of outtakes from the film and other gags with the cast.

Now head back to the main menu, and use the Right Arrow on the remote until the small New Line Cinema logo (on the right of the screen) is illuminated. Press Enter to be taken to a credits screen, and press Enter again over "JVC digital Cybercam" to watch a short commercial with Buzz Aldrin—the second man on the moon (just behind Neil Armstrong)—promoting the JVC Cybercam digital camcorder.

Lastly, from the main menu, select "Features" and then "Jupiter II Crew." You'll find a hidden trailer to the film *Dark City* on the fifth page of William Hurt's biography. Press Enter to play it. Same goes for Mimi Rogers' entry— on the third and final page of her bio, you'll find a trailer to *Austin Powers: International Man of Mystery*.

M*A*S*H

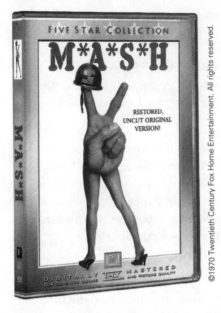

20th Century Fox

Released 1970

Directed by Robert Altman

Starring Donald Sutherland, Elliott Gould, Tom Skerritt

In this blockbuster movie that spawned the beloved '70s TV series of the same name, *M*A*S*H* observes the hilarious antics of three Korean War army surgeons at their Mobile Army Surgical Hospital (MASH).

Insert the first disc of this two-DVD set, and from the main menu, scroll down once and select "Special Features." Now scroll down four times until the THX logo is highlighted and press the Right Arrow. A small yellow helicopter will appear on the screen. Press Enter to watch an entertaining and extended Spanish trailer to the film.

Also, from the main menu on both discs, select some of the signs on the right side of the screen (such as "Officer's Mess" and "Operating Theater") to be treated to various audio clips from the film. The two DVDs contain a total of about ten clips.

Did You Know?

Director Robert Altman's son, Mike Altman, wrote the lyrics to the classic theme song for this film—at age 14!

Hawkeye's Famous M*A*S*H Extra-Dry Martini Recipe

The following is Hawkeye's Famous M*A*S*H Extra-Dry Martini Recipe that's "guaranteed to put some Seoul in your Korea." This recipe was concocted by Fox Home Video and used as a promotion for the launch of the season one box set:

Ingredients:

- 1 Bottle Gin
- 1 Bottle Vermouth

Additional Items Needed:

- 1 Hypodermic Needle
- 1 Martini Glass
- 1 Jar Of Olives (If In Korea, Please Contact "Trapper" John McIntyre)
- 1 Official Camouflage Army Canteen

1. Insert hypodermic needle into opening of bottle of vermouth.
2. Remove a minute amount of vermouth.
3. Empty contents of needle into martini glass.
4. Swirl vermouth in glass. Be sure to cover all surface area of glass.
5. Empty contents of glass.
6. Pour gin into glass.
7. Add olive.
8. Enjoy beverage.
9. Repeat steps 1–7 until content.
10. Pass out.

Mad Max: Special Edition

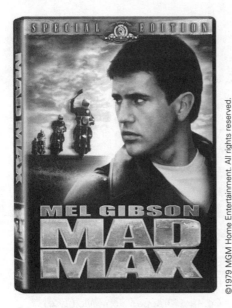

MGM

Released 1979

Directed by George Miller

Starring Mel Gibson

In Mel Gibson's second film—about a grim, lawless society in the near future—his character, Max Rockatowsky, seeks revenge for the murder of his family by a savage motorcycle gang.

There are a few cool surprises buried deep within the "Special Edition" of this DVD.

On the main menu, press the Up Arrow three times until the big red words "Mad Max" appear at the top of the screen. Press Enter to view five hidden sections about the cars from the film: the Black Interceptor, Yellow Pursuit, Yellow Interceptor (1), Yellow Interceptor (2), and The Night Rider.

Each entry features a thorough description (including year and model, and where in the movie it appeared) and three images from the movie (totaling 15).

Here's another egg: on the same page, highlight the word "Yellow Interceptor (1)," but do not press Enter just yet. Instead, tap the Left Arrow, and the headlights on the three cars in the picture will turn red. Now press Enter to read some info on Goose's '77 Kawasaki motorcycle in the film, with three action shots as well.

Did You Know?

In the U.S. version of the film, Gibson's voice was dubbed over because the producers were concerned American audiences wouldn't understand his thick Aussie accent.

Made: Special Edition

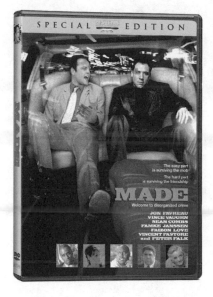

Artisan Entertainment

Released 2001

Directed by Jon Favreau

Starring Jon Favreau, Vince Vaughn, Sean "P. Diddy" Combs, Famke Janssen, Faizon Love, Vincent Pastore, Peter Falk

In this crime comedy, two lifelong friends and smalltime hustlers are hired by mob boss Max (Peter Falk) to go to New York for a "job," in order to prove themselves.

Pop in the DVD, and from the main menu, enter the section "Special Features," and then select "More Made Footage." Once inside, select "Alternate Scenes"; the last entry on this page is "Double Cross." Scroll down to highlight the words, and press the Left Arrow. A small *M* will appear on the screen.

Press Enter and nothing will happen—but don't worry—you need to spell the word "Made."

Now press the Left Arrow, and a pink *A* will appear. Press Enter. Now press the Right Arrow, and the *D* will appear; press Enter. Press the Left Arrow on the remote and an *E* will appear. Now press Enter again and nothing will happen until you press the Right Arrow one more time. The entire word "MADE" will now be spelled out—click Enter to view a much sexier version of the bachelor party lap-dance scene from the movie (Warning: nudity).

If you're having trouble accessing this racy scene, there's another way to view it. Select the words "Double Cross" from the "Alternate Scene" section, and when this video begins, press the right Skip button on the remote once to launch the lap-dance sequence.

Magnolia

New Line Cinema

Released 1999

Directed by Paul Thomas Anderson

Starring Jeremy Blackman, Tom Cruise, Melinda Dillon, Philip Baker Hall, Philip Seymour Hoffman, Ricky Jay, William H. Macy, Alfred Molina, Julianne Moore, John C. Reilly, Jason Robards, Melora Walters

By coincidence or divine intervention, the lives of nine people cross paths in this extraordinary tale of courage, guilt, remorse, love, faith, and fate.

Insert the first of two DVDs, and wait until the main menu appears. One of your choices will be "Set Up"—select this and then choose the "Color Bars" section. You'll see those familiar colored bars ("as seen on TV"), but wait for a few seconds until the bars disappear. Now kick back and enjoy close to ten minutes of bloopers from the film, including some comical Tom Cruise mess-ups.

Did You Know?

Allegedly, director Paul Thomas Anderson wrote most of the script while at actor William H. Macy's cabin in Vermont because he was too afraid to face a snake outside.

Mallrats: Collector's Edition

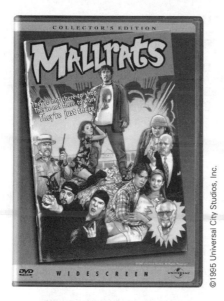

©1995 Universal City Studios, Inc.

Universal Pictures

Released 1995

Directed by Kevin Smith

Starring Shannen Doherty, Jeremy London, Jason Lee, Claire Forlani

This cult classic takes place—where else—at the mall, where two friends, T.S. Quint (Jeremy London) and Brodie Bruce (Jason Lee), decide to hang out after being dumped by their respective girlfriends. To help win them back, their dysfunctional buds, Jay (Jason Mewes) and Silent Bob (Kevin Smith), come up with a surefire scheme.

From the main menu, select "Bonus Materials" and then choose "Deleted Scenes." Now press the Right Arrow four times until the robot's eyes turn red. Then press Enter.

Smith and a colleague will tease you and say, "If you're here, you probably thought this was going to be an Easter egg, something hidden. You think you're so clever?"

Smith then says there is no such egg here, and to go and buy some Jay and Bob merchandise instead!

Did You Know?

Mallrats is but one of Kevin Smith's films that are all linked to one another in some way, shape or form. In particular, *Clerks* (1994), *Mallrats* (1995), *Chasing Amy* (1997), *Dogma* (1999), and *Jay and Silent Bob Strike Back* (2001) are all part of Smiths' "View Askewniverse" series, complete with interconnected characters, locations, and events. Visit www.viewaskew.com for more information.

Man on the Moon

Universal Studios

Released 1999

Directed by Milos Forman

Starring Jim Carrey, Danny DeVito, Courtney Love, Paul Giamatti

Jim Carrey, who won a Golden Globe award for this film, chronicles the personal and professional life of the late eccentric comic, Andy Kaufman (best known for his role in the '70s sitcom *Taxi*). Based on a true story, *Man on the Moon* delves into the rise and fall of Kaufman's career, as well as his close relationships with his manager, George Shapiro (Danny DeVito); his best friend and partner, Bob Zmuda (Paul Giamatti); and his love interest, Lynne Margulies (Courtney Love).

Fans of Kaufman will certainly relish the hidden extras on this DVD.

From the main menu, scroll up to "Bonus Materials" and click Enter. Scroll to the bottom of the page to the word "Andy," and press Enter to peruse through a short biography on this unconventional comedian/actor/musician.

If you notice, many pages of this biography include a small black-and-white picture of Kaufman, so press the Up Arrow, and an orange lining will encircle the image. Press Enter to watch some entertaining video clips of Kaufman in action.

The section contains six clips.

Mars Attacks!

Warner Bros.

Released 1996

Directed by Tim Burton

Starring Jack Nicholson, Glenn Close, Annette Bening, Pierce Brosnan, Danny DeVito

Tim Burton's sci-fi spoof on '50s UFO invasion movies features an all-star cast: Jack Nicholson, Glenn Close, Pierce Brosnan, Tom Jones, Danny DeVito, Annette Bening, Martin Short, Michael J. Fox, and Sarah Jessica Parker.

Why did these big-brained aliens come to Earth? For wanton destruction, of course. And what better place to start than Las Vegas.

There's a small but humorous Easter egg to be found on the DVD.

From the main menu, select the "Soundtracks" option, and you'll see the familiar choices: English, Spanish, French…and Martian!

Scroll down and press Enter over the "Martian" soundtrack option, and a new screen will appear with some graphics and funny Martian dialogue.

Did You Know?

Here's a small trivia tidbit: Did you know the sound effects used for the ray guns were taken from Orson Welles' *The War of the Worlds*?

The Matrix

Warner Bros.

Released 1999

Directed by Andy Wachowski, Larry Wachowski

Starring Keanu Reeves, Laurence Fishburne, Carrie-Anne Moss, Hugo Weaving

Easily one of the most influential sci-fi films in recent memory (especially in the special effects department), *The Matrix* stars Keanu Reeves as a savvy computer hacker who learns about the true nature of reality. He joins rebels Morpheus (Laurence Fishburne) and Trinity (Carrie-Anne Moss) as they attempt to overthrow the Matrix, a computer that runs the "world" as we know it.

From the main menu, scroll down and select "Special Features." Choose "The Dream World." See that little red pill on the bottom left of the screen? Good. Scroll down and click on it to watch a hidden six-minute documentary entitled "What is Bullet Time?"

While still in the "Special Features" area, click on the tab entitled "Cast & Crew." Select "Written and Directed by The Wachowski Brothers." You'll see another red pill, this time on the bottom right of the screen. Move to it and press Enter to view an 11-minute featurette, "What Is Concept?"

Lastly, also in the "Special Features" menu, select "Continue," and on the second page, select the "Follow the White Rabbit" mode. When you choose this, you can watch the entire movie again, but this time, whenever you see a white rabbit, select the icon to be taken to even more secrets embedded on the disc.

The Easter eggs hidden in The Matrix aren't too hard to find—after all a white rabbit and red pill are good clues taken right from the film—but they're rewarding nonetheless.

The Matrix Revisited

Warner Bros.

Released 2001 (based on *The Matrix,* 1999)

Directed by Josh Oreck

Starring Keanu Reeves, Laurence Fishburne, Carrie-Anne Moss, Hugo Weaving

Just like *The Matrix* DVD, this documentary disc also contains a few clever Easter eggs.

Enter the "Languages" section from the main menu, and then press the Left Arrow on the remote. A small phone booth will appear in the middle of the screen. Press Enter to play all 41 songs from this documentary. (You can listen to them in order as they're presented here or choose individual songs.)

Want to see the original (and extended) theatrical trailer to *The Matrix*? In this music jukebox area, stay on the screen highlighting songs 11 through 20. Press the Right Arrow on the remote, and a bullet will appear near Neo (Keanu Reeves). Now press Enter.

There are more eggs on this disc. To access them, enter the "Go Further" section from the main menu, and press the Right Arrow to watch clips of the "Woman in Red," Hugo Weaving's surgery, and Keanu Reeve's training.

Me, Myself & Irene

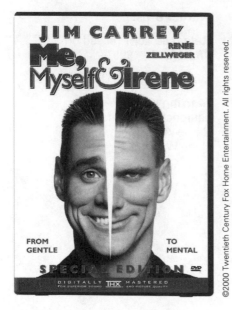

20th Century Fox

Released 2000

Directed by Bobby Farrelly, Peter Farrelly

Starring Jim Carrey, Renée Zellweger

In this hilarious comedy, Jim Carrey plays schizophrenic Rhode Island state trooper Charlie Baileygates, who falls in love with a wanted woman, Irene P. Waters (Renée Zellweger).

From the main menu, select "Bonus Features" and then choose "Deleted Scenes." Now press the Down Arrow until Carrey's face appears at the bottom of the screen. Press Enter and enjoy this collection of hilarious outtakes from the film.

Also, try this—go back to the main menu, and let the video clips play, but don't touch the remote for a minute or so. You'll then be asked if you need to take your medication. If you choose "Thanks, I Almost Forgot," it'll kick you back out to the main menu. However, if you click "No Thanks, I Feel Fine," the screen will shake and then "crazier" red menus, taunting music, and new video clips will appear!

The Mexican

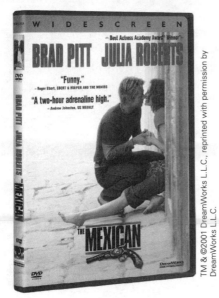

TM & ©2001 DreamWorks L.L.C., reprinted with permission by DreamWorks L.L.C.

DreamWorks Pictures

Released 2001

Directed by Gore Verbinski

Starring Brad Pitt, Julia Roberts, James Gandolfini

This romantic comedy stars Brad Pitt as Jerry Welbach, who is torn between his girlfriend Samantha Barzel (Julia Roberts) and mob boss Winston Baldry (James Gandolfini). Welbach promises Barzel he'll end his criminal ways but must go to Mexico for Baldry to retrieve a priceless—and allegedly cursed—antique pistol known as "The Mexican."

From the main menu of this DVD, scroll down twice and select the "Special Features" page. Then scroll down to the "Cast" section, and choose the biography for "Brad Pitt."

Beside his name at the top of the screen, you'll notice a filmstrip. Press the Up Arrow on the DVD remote, and the filmstrip will turn from red to yellow. Press Enter to watch a lengthy deleted scene where Welbach (Pitt) is attempting to call Baldry (Roberts) from a Mexican pay phone, but gets her answering machine instead.

Monkeybone

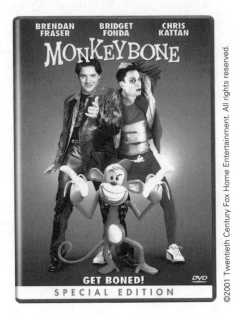

20th Century Fox

Released 2001

Directed by Henry Selick

Starring Brendan Fraser, Bridget Fonda, Chris Kattan

In this comedy, cartoonist Stu Miley (Brendan Fraser) falls into a coma, unleashing Monkeybone, his racy alter-ego who is determined to wreak havoc on the real world. Miley must catch Monkeybone before his sister pulls the plug on him, while avoiding Death (portrayed by Whoopi Goldberg!).

The film combines stop-motion animation with live-action to deliver a unique visual experience.

OK, now on to the Easter egg…

From the main menu, select "Language Selection" and once inside, press the Right Arrow. A monkey holding a sign will appear advising, "Press Play to See the Organ Harvest."

Press Enter to be treated to a special behind-the-scenes video showing how the organ-donor scene in the movie was achieved.

Monster's Ball

Lions Gate Films

Released 2001

Directed by Marc Forster

Starring Billy Bob Thornton, Heath Ledger, Halle Berry

Hank Grotowski (Billy Bob Thorton) is a bigoted prison guard who reexamines his beliefs after falling in love with Leticia Musgrove (Halle Berry), the wife of a recently executed black prisoner.

Berry took home the coveted "Best Actress in a Leading Role" Oscar at the 2002 Academy Awards for her performance in this film.

From the main menu, highlight the words "Play Movie," but don't press Enter just yet. Instead, press the Up Arrow, and a secret Lion's Gate Entertainment logo will appear on the screen. Press Enter to be treated to a trio of trailers to other Lion's Gate films: *Chelsea Walls, The Rules of Attraction,* and *The Cat's Meow.*

Now go back to the main menu and select "Special Features." Once inside, press the Up Arrow and a small logo will appear for American Cinematheque. Press Enter to watch a lengthy preview of *Everything Put Together* (2000), another film by director Marc Forster.

Moulin Rouge

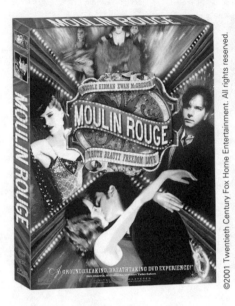

20th Century Fox

Released 2001

Directed by Baz Luhrmann

Starring Nicole Kidman, Ewan McGregor

One of the most memorable (and refreshingly distinctive) musicals of our time, *Moulin Rouge* takes place at the turn of the 20th century in Paris, where a lonely poet, Christian (Ewan McGregor), falls for the beautiful Satine (Nicole Kidman), the sexy star of the Moulin Rouge. A whopping 15 eggs are on *Moulin Rouge,* all on the second disc.

Ready? Here we go:

1. Click "More" to enter the second page. Press the Right Arrow five times, and a red fairy appears on the theater screen. Now press Enter to be taken to a silly dancing scene performed by the character Harold Zidler (played by Jim Broadbent).

2. From the main menu, select "The Cutting Room" and then click Enter. Tap the Right Arrow four times until a red windmill appears. Click Enter to view an outtake of McGregor serenading Kidman to Elton John's "Your Song."

3. Head to the submenu entitled "The Dance," and then select "The Dance" again. Highlight the section "A Word from Baz" and press the Right Arrow. A green fairy will appear beside this section. Press Enter to view a dance rehearsal.

4. Head to the submenu "The Design," and once inside, select "Costume Design" and then enter the section "A Courtesan's Wardrobe." Scroll to the fourth page, press the Up Arrow, and a green fairy will appear. Press Enter to watch another outtake with Kidman and McGregor.

5. Under the "The Music" submenu, scroll down and enter "The Lady Marmalade Phenomenon." Press the Right Arrow three times, and a red windmill will appear at the bottom of the screen. Press Enter for a scene with Baz driving in a car.

6. From the main menu, select "The Design" and once inside, press "18" on the DVD remote, and then "99" (1899 is the year the movie begins), and this'll launch some behind-the-scenes makeup footage of men getting their nipples brushed with rouge!

7. Stay in "The Design" and choose "Set Design" from the list. Now click on "Spectacular Spectacular," and scroll to the second page (with the words "Spectacular Spectacular" written on the picture). Once here, press the Up Arrow, and press Enter to watch Baz introduce you to the magic of the soundstage.

8. While still in the "Set Design" area, choose "The Gothic Tower," and scroll over to the fifth page (using the Skip buttons). Press the Up Arrow and then press Enter for even more rehearsal footage with Kidman (in sexy glasses!) playing a joke on McGregor.

9. From the "Set Design" submenu, select "The Bohemians," and scroll over to the fifth page. Press the Up Arrow and press Enter to highlight the windmill. This will launch a cancan rehearsal.

10. From the main menu, select "Marketing" and then head to "Photo Gallery." Scroll down once to highlight the name "Mary Ellen Mark," and then press the Right Arrow; a red windmill will appear. Press Enter to view a wardrobe fitting with John Leguizamo (who played Henri de Toulouse Lautrec in the film).

11. From the main menu, select "The Stars"; once this video clip ends, press "9" and then "17" on the DVD remote to access a hidden scene with three bagpipers—a surprise Luhrmann arranged for McGregor as a going-away present.

12. While still in "The Stars," press the Up Arrow when over Leguizamo's portrait, and a green fairy will appear. Press Enter to see Leguizamo dressed as an Indian sitar instrument.

13. From the main menu, select "This Story is About..." and select the third entry, "Old Storylines & Script Comparisons." Once inside, press the Right Arrow five times, and a green fairy will appear on the screen. Press Enter to see Luhrmann wielding a hammer as a joke.

14. From the main menu, select "The Dance" and then enter the section "Choreography." Once inside, press the Right Arrow three times, and a red windmill will appear to the right of the words "Main Menu." Press Enter to watch Luhrmann dance around a stage.

15. From the main menu, select "The Design" and then click on the last entry: "Smoke and Mirrors." Once inside, press "5" and then "18" on the DVD remote, and this'll launch another rehearsal clip—this time of all the Parisian men throwing their top hats in the air at the club.

Did You Know?

This award-winning movie took 188 days to shoot, with 650 extras and over 750 crew members.

The enormous elephant (which was over 32 feet tall) used in the film took over two months to build...but only two days to destroy.

Cat Stevens' "Father & Son" was the only song that was refused permission to be included in the movie—allegedly, it was refused on religious grounds.

There were over 60 make-up and hair crew on the movie. And get this—over 85 colored wigs were designed and custom-made in Rome.

Nicole Kidman broke her rib twice while shooting the film. The first time was during preproduction, and the second was during filming while being fitted for a corset.

The Mummy: Ultimate Edition

©1999 Universal Studios

Universal Studios

Released 1999

Directed by Stephen Sommers

Starring Brendan Fraser, Rachel Weisz

Three thousand years ago, the priest Imhotep (Arnold Vosloo) was tortured and mummified alive for sleeping with the Pharaoh's girlfriend. Now, in 1923, he has returned to wreak havoc. This ancient curse is accidentally unleashed as adventurous French foreign legionnaire Richard O'Connell (Brendan Fraser) and a band of treasure hunters discover the lost city of Hamunaptra.

Music lovers will enjoy the Easter egg embedded on this "Ultimate Edition" DVD of *The Mummy*.

From the disc's main menu, enter the section entitled "Languages," and wait for a moment until the animation finishes. Now turn up the volume, and put your feet on the coffee table—you can listen to Jerry Goldsmith's movie soundtrack in its entirety.

Here's one more egg: Select the "Bio" section for actors Brendan Fraser and Arnold Vosloo to uncover secret trailers to the films *Darkman II* and *Gods and Monsters*.

The Mummy Returns

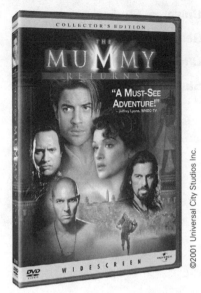

Universal Pictures

Released 2001

Directed by Stephen Sommers

Starring Brendan Fraser, Rachel Weisz, John Hannah, Arnold Vosloo, Oded Fehr, Patricia Velazquez, Dwayne "The Rock" Johnson

This is the second film in this action/adventure series back by popular demand. This time around, an ancient legacy of terror is unleashed when the accursed mummy, Imhotep (Arnold Vosloo), is resurrected along with the Scorpion King (Dwayne Johnson). Back to save the world are Rick O'Connell (Brendan Fraser) and his wife, Evie (Rachel Weisz).

From the DVD's main menu, scroll up to the "Bonus Materials" section, and once inside, enter the second page of features by pressing Enter over the word "More."

One of the entries will be "Egyptology 201"—select it and then choose the first entry, "An In-Depth Look at Mummification." Now press the Right Arrow on the DVD remote twice until a scorpion symbol turns red on the screen. Press Enter to watch a two-minute video about a 1994 mummification at the University of Maryland!

Another secret goodie is also on the second page of "Bonus Materials." This time, press the Up Arrow twice, and the hieroglyphs above the word "Menu" will turn red. Press Enter to view the DVD credits.

The Ninth Gate

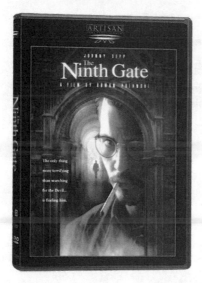

Artisan

Released 1999

Directed by Roman Polanski

Starring Johnny Depp, Lena Olin, Frank Langella, James Russo, Jack Taylor, Emmanuelle Seigner

In this gothic thriller, Dean Corso (Johnny Depp) is a rare-book dealer who is hired to locate the last remaining copies of *The Nine Gates of the Shadow Kingdom,* a manuscript that can summon the devil himself.

From the disc's main menu, head over to "Special Features," and once inside, highlight the word "Trailers" without pressing Enter. Instead, tap the Left Arrow and the words "TV Spot 1" will appear on the lower-left of the screen. Press Enter to view this *Ninth Gate* television commercial.

Now head back to "Special Features," and click the small arrow at the bottom to access the second page of bonus materials. Now scroll down to the bottom, and enter the section "Gallery Of Satanic Drawings." Once inside, click the little arrows at the bottom to get to the fourth gate, known as "Chance is not the same for all." On the second drawing/page of the fourth gate, the word "AT" will appear on the screen. Press the Up Arrow and the word will turn green. Press Enter to watch another TV spot for *The Ninth Gate.*

Head back to the second page of "Special Features," and select "Production Notes," second from the top. Once inside, scroll through to the tenth (and final) page, and then tap the Up Arrow. The words "TV Spot" will appear in the image. Press Enter to watch another promo for the film.

The last trailer for this movie is in the "Cast and Crew" section, on the second page of "Special Features." Head to the second page of cast and crew members (by selecting the little arrow at the bottom of the screen), and then choose "Michael Cheyko." On the third page of his bio, the word "AT" will appear on the screen again. Press the Up Arrow and the word will turn yellow. Now press Enter to watch a fourth trailer to the film.

O Brother, Where Art Thou?

Universal Pictures

Released 2000

Directed by Joel Coen

Starring George Clooney, John Turturro

In this tale, loosely based on Homer's *Odyssey*, three convicts escape a chain gang in the 1920s and set out in search of treasure. While on the run from the law, these mismatched criminals—the charming Ulysses (George Clooney), the hot-tempered Pete (John Turturro), and the slow-witted Delmar (Tim Blake Nelson)—inadvertently become a popular country music troupe along the way to finding their fortune.

The undocumented extra on this DVD is easy to find—simply pop in the disc, and don't touch anything at the main menu.

The instrumental music track that plays in its entirety in the background is a little-known tune from the *O Brother, Where Art Thou?* production featurette. Enjoy!

The Peacemaker

TM & ©1996 DreamWorks L.L.C., reprinted with permission by DreamWorks L.L.C.

DreamWorks Pictures

Released 1997

Directed by Mimi Leder

Starring George Clooney, Nicole Kidman

In this white-knuckle thriller, Colonel Thomas Devoe (George Clooney) and Dr. Julia Kelly (Nicole Kidman) put aside their personal differences to join forces and stop a terrorist from stealing nuclear weapons.

From the disc's main menu, select "Special Features" and then choose the "Cast & Crew" option. Now select the bio of Clooney, which includes a secret interview snippet. To access it, press the Up Arrow, and Clooney's picture at the top of the screen will spawn a subtle green glow. Press Enter. Clooney talks about how he got the part for this film and why he accepted this role.

Now try the same thing for Kidman's bio and director Mimi Leder's bio (press the Up Arrow for each) to view even more behind-the-scenes interviews.

Planet of the Apes

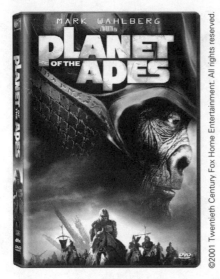

20th Century Fox

Released 2001

Directed by Tim Burton

Starring Mark Wahlberg, Tim Roth, Helena Bonham Carter

In this remake of the popular '60s sci-fi film and '70s TV series, *Planet of the Apes* takes place in 2029, when an American astronaut Capt. Leo Davidson (Mark Wahlberg) crash lands on a strange planet inhabited by talking apes.

Pop in the first disc of this two-DVD set, and from the main menu, select "Special Features" and then choose "Commentaries." Now press the Down Arrow twice, and a red monkey will illuminate in the middle of the screen. Press Enter to watch a special commentary of the movie—in ape language!

Cute, but not as interesting as the second egg on this DVD.

In the last scene in the movie, where Davidson (Wahlberg) crash lands back on Earth and is standing in front of the General Thade memorial, click Enter when he's staring at the statue. A featurette will immediately launch, discussing the making of the sculpture.

Also, go back to the "Special Features" section from the main menu, and enter the "Cast & Crew Profiles" area. Once inside, select "Cast" and then enter the bio for "Estella Warren" (who plays Daena in the film). Now press the Up Arrow, and the arrow below her picture will turn orange. Press Enter to be treated to Warren's first audition for the part.

First audition tapes for both Erick Avari ("Tival") and Luke Eberl ("Birn") can be accessed in the same way.

Lastly, go back to the main menu and select "Language Selection" at the bottom of the screen. Scroll down to highlight the words "Resume Film," and instead of pressing Enter, tap the Right Arrow. A monkey's head in red will appear in the corner; press Enter to read the DVD credits.

Practical Magic

Warner Bros.

Released 1998

Directed by Griffin Dunne

Starring Sandra Bullock, Nicole Kidman

It's not easy being a witch. Just ask sisters Sally and Gillian Owens (Sandra Bullock and Nicole Kidman, respectively), cursed to have all the men they fall in love with sent to an early grave. With some "practical magic" taught by their aunts, perhaps they can put an end to this centuries-old curse.

Insert the second side of the disc ("Special Features"), and from the main menu, go to the "Special Features" section. Scroll to the middle of the screen, where the word "Cauldron" appears. Press Enter and a screen with some herbs will appear, such as rosemary, mint, lavender, and others.

The goal is to brew a secret potion like Sally and Gillian did in the film, by selecting the right ingredients in the correct order. (Hint: Not all ingredients are needed, and clues to the right herbs are given in the other areas of this DVD.)

Successfully adding the ingredients will open two enjoyable documentaries. One is a six-minute film entitled "Making Magic," and the other is "Casting the Spell," a nine-minute short film on the cast, story, and the making of the film.

The Princess Bride: Special Edition

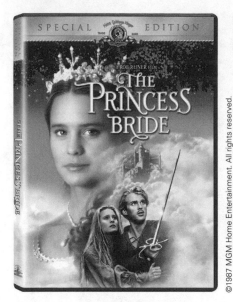

MGM

Released 1987

Directed by Rob Reiner

Starring Robin Wright, Cary Elwes, Mandy Patinkin, Billy Crystal

Fantasy meets comedy in Rob Reiner's classic tale about the beautiful Buttercup (Robin Wright), who is held captive and will be forced to marry a detestable prince. Little does she know that her childhood sweetheart Westley (Cary Elwes) is determined to rescue her (though he's supposed to be dead), with the aid of two zany companions.

From the disc's main menu, press Up Arrow on the remote, and a turquoise gem will glow at the top of the screen. Press Enter to be taken to another screen with nothing but the heads of eight cast members.

Now use the Up, Down, Left, and Right Arrows to navigate among the heads; pressing Enter will cause the selected head to grow even bigger, and a sound bite from that character will play.

Also on this screen are two other gems on each side of the words "Main Menu" at the bottom. Use the remote keys to highlight them and they'll turn purple. Press Enter to hear more lines from the film.

Requiem for a Dream

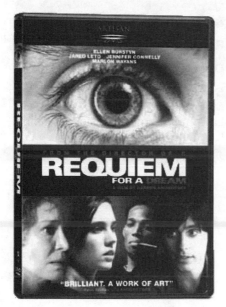

Artisan Entertainment

Released 2000

Directed by Darren Aronofsky

Starring Ellen Burstyn, Jared Leto, Jennifer Connelly, Marlon Wayans, Christopher McDonald

This disturbing tale examines the lives of four Coney Island residents grappling with varying forms of addiction, denial, and depression. Ellen Burstyn's outstanding performance as a TV-obsessed widow won her a nomination for Best Actress in a Leading Role at the 2001 Academy Awards.

As with most other Artisan DVDs, the *Requiem for a Dream* disc features a few clever Easter eggs.

From the main menu, press the Up Arrow or Down Arrow on the remote until the words "Hear Tappy's Amazing Life Story!" are illuminated in yellow. Press Enter to view the complete five-minute infomercial from the movie.

Also, inside the "Chapter Index," use the Right Arrow to move over to the "Chapters 21 to 24" section. Press the Up Arrow twice to watch a never-before-released part of Tappy's show on how to change your life. Here, fans of the film can find out what rule 3 was…though you may not like the sound of it.

Reservoir Dogs

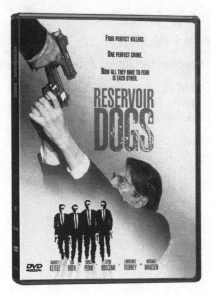

Artisan

Released 1992

Directed by Quentin Tarantino

Starring Harvey Keitel, Tim Roth, Michael Madsen, Steve Buscemi, Lawrence Tierney, Christopher Penn, Quentin Tarantino

In *Reservoir Dogs,* his first feature film, Quentin Tarantino turned Hollywood upside down with his unique direction (placing events out of chronological order and merging separate stories into one), not to mention his irreverent screenplay and memorable characters! Who could forget Mr. White, Mr. Pink, and Mr. Brown?

There's a clever—and rewarding—Easter egg on the original DVD release of *Reservoir Dogs.*

Pop in the disc, and from the main menu, head to the "Special Features" section. A picture of the cop tied to a chair in the warehouse will be on the screen. Instead of scrolling through these options, click the Right Arrow on the DVD remote, and an ear will appear. Press Enter to watch a 20-minute interview with director and writer Tarantino.

Rocky

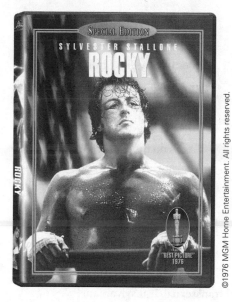

MGM

Released 1976

Directed by John G. Avildsen

Starring Sylvester Stallone

Rocky "The Italian Stallion" Balboa (Sylvester Stallone) is a small-time boxer who gets the chance to step into the ring with the heavyweight champ, Apollo Creed (Carl Weathers). With the help of his manager, Mickey Goldmill (Burgess Meredith), and his love interest, Adrian (Talia Shire), Rocky is determined to prove he can go the distance.

On the 25th anniversary edition DVD (also found in the *Rocky Box Set*), there's a humorous short film hidden within.

Simply pop in the disc and from the main menu, tap the Up Arrow on the remote. The words "Rocky" will illuminate toward the top of the screen. Now press Enter to watch an amusing clip entitled "Rocky Meets Stallone," where the actor Sylvester Stallone has a conversation with Rocky Balboa about what to do following the success of these boxing movies.

Did You Know?

Allegedly, Stallone wrote this script in just three days!

Sylvester Stallone was a poor, out of work actor when he wrote the screenplay for *Rocky*. Still, he refused to sell his script unless he was cast as the lead character.

123

The Rocky Horror Picture Show

20th Century Fox

Released 1975

Directed by Jim Sharman

Starring Tim Curry, Susan Sarandon, Barry Bostwick, Richard O'Brien

Let's do the "Time Warp" again—this time, on DVD.

This cult classic is based on the hit UK musical where a naive engaged couple—Brad (Barry Bostwick) and Janet (Susan Sarandon)—get lost on a rainy night and end up at a bizarre mansion crawling with extraterrestrial transsexual Transylvanians!

There are two cuts of the movie (U.S. and UK), but there's a hidden third version, too.

Pop in the first disc, and select either version of the film. From the main menu, scroll down to highlight the words "Scene Selection" (at the bottom of the screen), but don't press Enter. Instead, tap the Left Arrow, and a pair of yellow lips will appear in the bottom-left corner of the screen.

Now press Enter for a special treat—Richard O'Brien's original script indicated that the beginning of the film was to be shot in black and white as an affectionate nod to *The Wizard of Oz*. The film would turn to color only once Brad and Janet entered the world of the Transylvanians. Alas, this was decided against for a number of reasons, but this DVD does feature this rare, third version of the film.

Press Enter to play the movie.

Alternatively, there's an option to read the DVD credits from this screen.

Also, as an interesting note, press the Display button on the DVD remote during any of these three versions, to find out which one you're watching. If you're in the first or second version, switching to *3* in the Display window will immediately launch the Easter egg version as a shortcut.

Romeo + Juliet: Special Edition

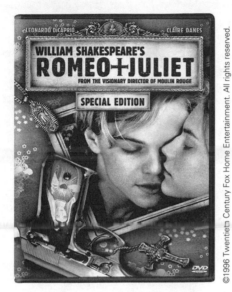

20th Century Fox

Released 1996

Directed by Baz Luhrmann

Starring Leonardo DiCaprio, Claire Danes

William Shakespeare's literary masterpiece is reborn in this brilliant remake, directed by visionary Baz Luhrmann (*Moulin Rouge, Strictly Ballroom*). This film chronicles the tragic love affair between Romeo (Leonardo DiCaprio) and Juliet (Claire Danes) and now takes place in Verona Beach during contemporary times.

The "Special Edition" DVD contains audio commentary by Luhrmann, various making-of featurettes, and other behind-the-scenes material.

From the disc's main menu, simply press the Up Arrow on the DVD remote, and the little heart at the top of the screen will illuminate yellow. Press Enter to read a few pages of the DVD credits, followed by a shortcut to the "Director's Gallery" and the six clips within.

The Royal Tenenbaums: The Criterion Collection

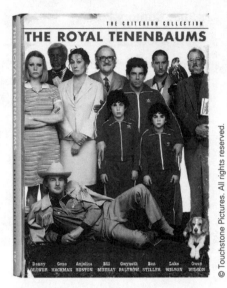

**Touchstone Pictures/
The Criterion Collection**

Released 2001

Directed by Wes Anderson

Starring Danny Glover, Gene Hackman, Anjelica Huston, Bill Murray, Gwyneth Paltrow, Ben Stiller, Luke Wilson, Owen Wilson

In one of the more distinctive and celebrated comedies of 2001, Royal Tenenbaum (Gene Hackman) makes an attempt to reunite with his estranged wife (Anjelica Houston) and dysfunctional yet brilliant children. Is it too little, too late? See for yourself in this feature-packed "Criterion Collection" edition DVD.

Oh yes, and there are two Easter eggs, too.

Insert the second DVD, and from the main menu, press the Up Arrow on the remote. A small on-screen arrow will point toward the words "The Criterion Collection" at the top of this page. Press Enter and Chas Tenenbaum (Ben Stiller) will take a break from shaving with his kids to welcome you to this special edition DVD.

Also on this second disc, select "Scrapbook" from the main menu and once inside, press the Down Arrow on the remote until the cursor points toward the Dalmatian mouse in the bottom left-hand corner of the screen. Press Enter to watch a silly deleted scene with Bill Murray goofing around.

Rush Hour

New Line Cinema

Released 1998

Directed by Brett Ratner

Starring Jackie Chan, Chris Tucker

The fastest kick in the East meets the biggest mouth in the West in this blockbuster comedy about two mismatched cops determined to rescue the daughter of a Chinese diplomat.

And guess what—there's a fantastic Easter egg to uncover on this DVD. Problem is, it's very well hidden, and probably easier to find using a DVD-ROM drive rather than a standard DVD player.

Here's how to do it:

Once inside your PC's DVD software, start the movie, head over to Chapter 3, and then access Title 4. As you'll see, there's an early (and amateur!) Brett Ratner film, *Evil Luke Lee*.

When you find it, the director will congratulate you for your efforts before pleading "please, please, please don't show this to anyone!" Ratner then explains what you're about to see before the lengthy, humorous film begins to play.

Also, from the main menu, scroll to the bottom of the screen, and the "Infinifilm" logo will be highlighted underneath the option for "Scene Selections." Press Enter and the logo will turn yellow before jumping to a DVD production credits screen.

Rush Hour 2

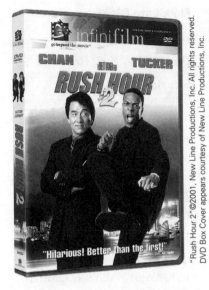

New Line Cinema

Released 2001

Directed by Brett Ratner

Starring Jackie Chan, Chris Tucker

In this successful sequel, LAPD Det. James Carter (Chris Tucker) travels to Hong Kong for a well-deserved vacation, but once again finds himself solving crime alongside the acrobatic Chief Inspector Lee (Jackie Chan).

Pop in the DVD, and from the main menu, choose "Select A Scene." Look at the chapter numbers at the bottom of the screen. All but two of these pages feature three different scenes to jump to.

The first page with only two scenes has scenes 7 and 8. Select this by pressing Enter over the numbers *7–8*, and one of the three video-clip entries will be blank except for a red dragon. Use the remote to navigate over to this dragon, and press Enter to enjoy a lengthy widescreen trailer to *Lord of the Rings: The Fellowship of the Ring,* complete in 5.1 digital sound!

Now go to sections 15 and 16, and instead of a red dragon, there's a large number *7.* Navigate over to it and press Enter to watch yet another anamorphic trailer for Peter Jackson's first *Lord of the Rings* feature film.

Lastly, go back to the main menu, press the Left Arrow on the DVD remote, and a small white "Infinifilm" logo will appear underneath the Chinese food take-out box. Press Enter to read the DVD production credits.

Did you Know?

Much of the movie takes place in the "Red Dragon" hotel, which was really the renovated "Desert Inn" in Las Vegas. The aging hotel was demolished in late 2001 after the movie was filmed. Director Brett Ratner's next film also happens to be named "Red Dragon," continuing the (mis)adventures of Dr. Hannibal "The Cannibal" Lecter (played by Anthony Hopkins).

Shallow Hal

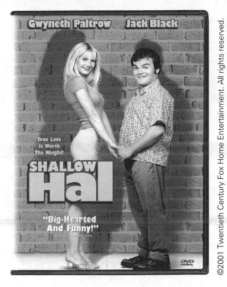

20th Century Fox

Released 2001

Directed by Bobby Farrelly, Peter Farrelly

Starring Gwyneth Paltrow, Jack Black, Jason Alexander

Directed by the same brothers who brought us *There's Something About Mary* (1998) and *Me, Myself & Irene* (2000), this "heavyweight" romantic comedy stars Hal Larson (Jack Black), a shallow skirt-chaser who, after being hypnotized by a self-help guru, only sees the inner beauty of women. Of course, he doesn't realize his gorgeous girlfriend Rosemary (Gwyneth Paltrow) is actually a 300-pound woman.

From the main menu of this DVD, choose the second menu, "Language Selection," and then scroll down four times and highlight the word "English" under the word "Captions & Subtitles."

Don't press Enter just yet—instead, press the Right Arrow, and a blue tail will appear on Jason Alexander's shadow. Now press Enter and it'll turn red, launching a "cheeky" demonstration of the tail special effects.

Shanghai Noon

Buena Vista Pictures

Released 2000

Directed by Tom Dey

Starring Jackie Chan, Owen Wilson, Lucy Liu

East meets West in this stunt-filled Western comedy starring Jackie Chan as a devoted Chinese Imperial Guard who travels to America to rescue a kidnapped princess (Lucy Liu). He joins up with a laid-back cowboy, played by Owen Wilson, on the run from the law.

From the main menu of this DVD, select "Bonus Materials" and then select "Shanghai Surprise." Here you'll find two fun video games that test your knowledge of the film.

The payoff for finishing these games successfully is two never-before-released clips: one is an animatic of the train crash sequence (one that didn't appear in the film), and the other is the memorable drinking scene—but this time around all of the Chinese spoken by Chon Wang (Chan) has English subtitles.

Showgirls

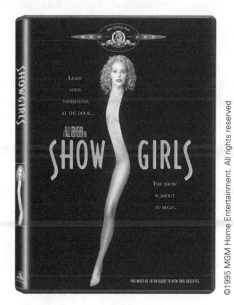

MGM

Released 1995

Directed by Paul Verhoeven

Starring Elizabeth Berkley, Kyle MacLachlan, Gina Gershon, Glenn Plummer, Robert Davi, Alan Rachins

In one of the more seductively controversial Hollywood films from the mid-'90s, Nomi Malone (Elizabeth Berkley) is determined to make it as a Las Vegas showgirl, but in doing so, gets a good look at Sin City's seedy underbelly.

There's some extra content packed onto this steamy DVD.

From the main menu, you'll notice an animated showgirl sign in flashing neon lights at the top of the screen. Each of the letters that make up the word "Showgirls" will play a hidden piece of dialogue from the film.

Here's how to access them: Use the Left Arrow or Right Arrow on the remote, and scroll across the various letters. Press Enter when on top of one the letters such as *S* or *G* to play an audio sound bite.

Shrek

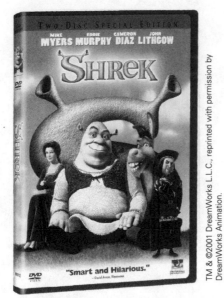

"Smart and Hilarious."
— David Ansen, Newsweek

TM & ©2001 DreamWorks L.L.C., reprinted with permission by DreamWorks Animation.

DreamWorks Pictures

Released 2001

Directed by Andrew Adamson, Vicky Jenson

Starring Mike Myers, Eddie Murphy, Cameron Diaz, John Lithgow

What do you get when you combine a reclusive ogre, a loudmouth donkey, a tiny-but-evil ruler, and a feisty princess with a lousy singing voice? The answer, of course, is *Shrek,* the incredibly successful computer-animated film.

As if the 11 hours of extra footage weren't enough on this two-disc set, it also contains two hidden eggs.

Pop in either of the two discs, and select the "Special Features" menu section. Now press the Up Arrow twice until the Gingerbread Man's buttons turn orange. Now press Enter to read a random Shrek "Fun Fact." Each time you visit this egg, you'll see a different fact.

A second egg is on the second disc. Navigate over to the word "Play," but don't press Enter just yet. Instead, press the Up Arrow and a musical note will illuminate orange. Now press Enter to view the side-splitting "Shrek in the Swamp Karaoke Dance Party." Well done!

This dance party video can also be seen simply by letting the movie roll past the credits.

The Simpsons: Season 1 Box Set

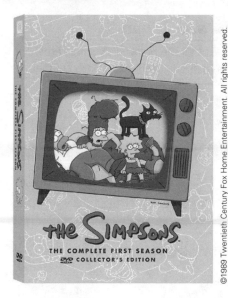

20th Century Fox

TV Series

Began 1989

Starring the voices of Dan Castellaneta, Julie Kavner, Nancy Cartwright, Yeardley Smith, Hank Azaria, Harry Shearer

The longest-running prime-time comedy in television history now has more than 300 episodes in the can, and this season-one box set is a real treat for fans of the show—despite it being a little rough around the edges.

Unless you've been living under a 1974 copy of *TV Guide*, you know *The Simpsons* is an animated series starring a dysfunctional family including a lazy and slow father (Homer), a nagging homemaker (Marge), an underachiever and troublemaker son (Bart), a smart loner (Lisa), and a baby who doesn't talk (Maggie).

Pop in the third disc of this three-DVD box set, and head to the section "Extra Features." Now go to the second page of features by clicking the "Next" tab. Once inside, select "Art of The Simpsons," and then scroll down to the words "Extra Features"—but don't press Enter. Instead, tap the Left Arrow and Bart's comic book will change to gray. Press Enter to view a collection of magazine covers featuring America's favorite cartoon family, including *TV Guide, Newsweek,* and *Entertainment Weekly*.

Now go back to the second page of "Extra Features." Highlight the words "'Some Enchanted Evening' Script" without pressing Enter. Now tap the Left Arrow, and Bart's shirt will change from orange to purple. Press Enter to watch a humorous 1990 TV news report on Bart's alleged negative influence on kids, including profane T-shirts bearing his image and catchphrases.

133

The Best TV Box Sets on DVD

It's not just movies on DVD we love—but all the beloved TV series are slowly making their way to a box set near you. Here are a dozen of the best to date:

1. The Simpsons
2. The Sopranos
3. Sex and the City
4. Friends
5. M*A*S*H
6. The X-Files
7. Star Trek: The Next Generation
8. The Complete Monty Python Flying Circus
9. Twin Peaks
10. The Larry Sanders Show
11. Roots
12. Saturday Night Live

The Sixth Sense

Buena Vista Entertainment

Released 1999

Directed by M. Night Shyamalan

Starring Bruce Willis, Haley Joel Osment, Olivia Williams, Toni Collette

In this suspenseful thriller, child psychologist Dr. Malcolm Crowe (Bruce Willis) begins to treat a young, frightened eight-year-old, Cole Sear (Haley Joel Osment), who believes he can see dead people. Thanks to its spine-tingling twist, *The Sixth Sense* became one of the most talked-about films of the past decade.

And guess what—this supernatural DVD has a little-known bonus gem.

From the disc's main menu, select the "Bonus Materials" tab, and then scroll down all the way and select "More." You should see a jewelry box at the bottom of this second "Bonus Materials" page. Scroll down and select it with your remote, and the lid will open, revealing a videotape with the writing "Knight's First Horror Film" on it.

As introduced by *The Sixth Sense* director, M. Night Shyamalan, this video was made when he was 11 years old. The clip is about a minute and a half. Enjoy!

Snow White and the Seven Dwarves: Platinum Edition

Disney Pictures

Released 1937

Directed by David Hand

Starring Adriana Caselotti, Harry Stockwell, Lucille La Verne, Moroni Olsen, Billy Gilbert, Pinto Colvig, Otis Harlan, Scotty Mattraw, Roy Atwell, Stuart Buchanan

Disney's revered animated masterpiece comes alive on DVD with this exhaustive two-disc collection.

Along with the digitally restored widescreen version of the film, the discs' special features include documentaries, galleries, games, a karaoke sing-along, and a new rendition of "Some Day My Prince Will Come," sung by Barbara Streisand.

A number of eggs are hidden, too.

Pop in the second "Bonus Features" DVD, and you'll notice this main menu screen has images representing the various sections instead of text. If you'd rather read the names of the sections, scroll down and highlight the cauldron in the bottom left. Now, instead of pressing Enter, press the Right Arrow and the apple will illuminate. Press Enter to change the main menu to text options instead of graphical ones.

Now go back to the main menu, and select the wishing-well text or image to enter the "History" and "Storyboard to Film Comparisons" submenu. Once inside the well, press the Left Arrow, and the words "DVD Credits" will appear. Press Enter to read the six pages of credits on the making of this double DVD.

And while it's not quite an egg, pop in either the first disc or the second, and don't do anything from the main menu. After awhile, the mirror will throw out random comments when he gets bored, such as "Hello, hello, is anyone home?", "Is it something I said?", or "Don't mind me—I'll just hang around 'til you decide."

The Sopranos: The Complete Second Season

HBO

TV Series

Began 1999

Starring James Gandolfini, Lorraine Bracco, Edie Falco, Michael Imperioli, Dominic Chianese, Vincent Pastore, Steve Van Zandt, Tony Sirico, Joseph Badalucco Jr., Robert Iler, Nancy Marchand, Jamie-Lynn Sigler, John Ventimiglia, Drea de Matteo, David Proval

This mega-successful HBO mob series is a raw look at the life of the fictional Mafia Capo Tony Soprano, whose real family is as dysfunctional as his professional one.

A lot of time, money, and effort went into creating this DVD box set, so if you want to view the hidden production credits for *The Sopranos: The Complete Second Season*, follow these simple instructions:

Pop in any of the four discs, and from the main menu, press the Right Arrow, and a red "HBO Home Video" logo will appear in the bottom-right corner of the screen. Press Enter to read who's responsible for the DVD's menu design and animation, production, and audio commentary.

South Park: Volume 4

Warner Bros.

Released 1999

Animated TV Series

Created by Trey Parker and Matt Stone

The controversial *South Park* TV cartoon series (and feature film) chronicles the wacky adventures of four foul-mouthed boys from South Park, Colorado: Stan, Kyle, Cartman, and Kenny.

Don't be fooled by the cute appearance of these third-graders—this disc is rated MA for "Mature." That is, it has content rated not appropriate for viewers under 18 years of age.

While not quite an Easter egg, there's a hidden surprise on this fourth volume of the popular show. Instead of four episodes—as promoted on the back of the DVD box—there are actually five. And the fifth is a rare one at that.

As introduced by South Park creators Matt Stone and Trey Parker, the episode is entitled "Terrance and Phillip: Not Without My Anus," which aired on April Fool's Day instead of the second part of a cliff-hanger.

Spawn

New Line Cinema

Released 1997

Directed by Mark A.Z. Dippé

Starring Michael Jai White, John Leguizamo, Martin Sheen, Theresa Randle, Nicol Williamson, D.B. Sweeney

From the mind of comic-book legend Todd McFarlane comes this superhuman tale of good vs. evil.

Insert the "Special Features" side of the DVD. From the main menu, select "More" and then choose "Spawn Soundtrack." You will see the words "Trip Like I Do" on the left of the screen. You can use the DVD remote to highlight these words, and then press Enter to watch a Crystal Method video—but there's a cool Easter egg here instead.

Highlight the words "Trip Like I Do," and then press the Right Arrow, and a picture of rocker Marilyn Manson will appear on the screen. Press Enter and a new screen with three doors will appear. Press Enter on either the right or left door, and an animated sequence will begin with creatures going out one door and in another. Do this four times and a new screen will appear with the movie's creepy clown.

Now press Enter over the middle door (with the words "Parental Advisory" on them) to launch a Marilyn Manson music video.

Remove the DVD, flip it over, and insert it. From the main menu, select the words "Scene Selections" at the bottom of the screen; instead of pressing Enter, press the Left Arrow, and the black New Line Cinema logo will turn green. Press Enter to read a "Special Thanks" screen and DVD production credits.

Speed: Five Star Collection

20th Century Fox

Released 1994

Directed by Jan de Bont

Starring Keanu Reeves, Dennis Hopper, Sandra Bullock

In this tense action thriller, Keanu Reeves plays Officer Jack Traven, a LAPD SWAT expert who must diffuse a bomb planted beneath a city bus that's set to explode if the vehicle's speed drops below 50 miles an hour. Traven is aided by one of the passengers, the gutsy Annie Porter (Sandra Bullock). Together, they must foil the efforts of a revenge-driven criminal, Howard Payne (Dennis Hopper).

Pop in the second of the two discs of this "Five Star Collection" DVD, and scroll up to the words "Action: Sequences"—but without pressing Enter just yet. Instead, tap the Left Arrow on the remote, and a small white bus will appear. Press Enter and scroll to the right a few screens until you find another bus icon. Now press Enter to watch the video clip on the "passenger-friendly" excerpt from *Speed*, in which the cargo jet explosion never occurred. This scene was omitted on the airline version of the film so it wouldn't upset passengers!

Star Trek—Original Series

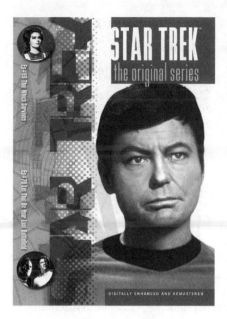

Paramount Pictures

TV series 1966–1969

Starring William Shatner, Leonard Nimoy, DeForest Kelley, James Doohan, Nichelle Nichols, George Takei, Walter Koenig

On each of the *Star Trek: The Original Series* discs, you'll find hidden TV trailers for that particular collection, and more.

Pop in the disc, and from the main menu, press the Up Arrow on the remote, and the Star Trek icon will turn from dark gray to silver. Press Enter to see four original trailers—two of which are for the episodes on that particular DVD; another two are trailers to promote the next two episodes in the series.

For example, episodes 21 and 22 (Volume 11 on DVD) will have secret trailers for episodes 21, 22, 23, and 24.

Now that's clever marketing!

Star Wars: The Phantom Menace

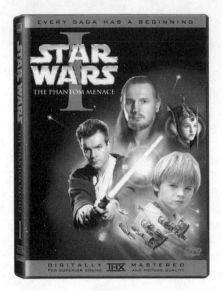

20th Century Fox/LucasFilm

Released 1999

Directed by George Lucas

Starring Liam Neeson, Ewan McGregor, Natalie Portman, Jake Lloyd, Ian McDiarmid

The force is back! Jedi Master Qui-Gon Jinn (Liam Neeson) and his apprentice, young Obi-Wan Kenobi (Ewan McGregor), are sent by the Chancellor of the Republic to the planet of Naboo to negotiate a heated trade dispute. The evil Senator Palpatine (and soon-to-be Emperor) is behind the strife and declares war on the innocent people of this world unless Queen "Padme Naberrie" Amidala (Natalie Portman) signs a treaty. The Queen and the annoying Nabooian creature Jar Jar Binks (Ahmed Best) are swiftly rescued by the two Jedis, but must take refuge on the planet Tatooine to find parts to repair their ship before organizing a counterattack. There they meet ten-year old Anakin Skywalker (Jake Lloyd), a.k.a. the young Darth Vader.

There are a number of clever eggs well-hidden on the DVD release of *Star Wars: Episode I—The Phantom Menace.*

The first (and finest) egg is a blooper reel of amusing outtakes. Here's how to access it:

On the first disc, go to the "Options" menu and type "1138" using your DVD remote. (One of Lucas' early films was *THX 1138.*) On some DVD players, you might have to press "10+," "1," and then "3" and "8." Sit back and enjoy an entertaining two-minute blooper reel.

Who knew R2D2 had such problems keeping upright?

The second egg enables you to choose which of the three planet themes to get when you pop in the DVD. (The choice is random otherwise.) Once the DVD is placed into the player and the red FBI warning comes on the screen, press the number 2 to be taken to the Tatooine theme. Alternatively, press the Audio button to launch the Naboo theme, or press "10+," "2," "2" for the Coruscant theme.

Insert the second DVD on this two-disc set, and from the main menu, select "Deleted Scenes and Documentaries" in the middle of the screen. Now choose "Deleted Scenes Only"; on the next page, "Complete Podrace Grid Sequence," push the Down Arrow so that the words "Doc Menu" turn yellow. Now press the Right Arrow, and a small yellow rectangle will appear. Press Enter to watch a two-and-a-half–minute "making-of" clip for the podrace sequence.

In the same "Deleted Scenes Only" page, click the Right Arrow to enter the page entitled "Extended Podrace Lap Two." Just like before, push the Down Arrow to highlight the words "Doc Menu," and press the Right Arrow on the DVD remote. Now press Enter to watch another featurette on the making of the podrace sequence.

StIgmata

MGM

Released 1999

Directed by Rupert Wainwright

Starring Patricia Arquette, Gabriel Byrne, Jonathan Pryce

Frankie Paige (Patricia Arquette) doesn't have faith in God. That is, until she begins to suffer the stigmata—bodily marks resembling the wounds of the crucified Christ. The Vatican's top investigator of paranormal activity, Father Kiernan (Gabriel Byrne), travels to America to see Paige and winds up in the middle of a global cover-up that could destroy the church.

The DVD contains a director's alternate ending, audio commentary, deleted scenes, a collectible eight-page booklet, trailers, videos, and an Easter egg.

From the disc's main menu, simply press the Up Arrow on the DVD remote, and a small circle above the word "Stigmata" will turn yellow. Press Enter to view a lengthy preproduction animatic of the chilling subway scene, using storyboard sketches.

Stir of Echoes

Artisan

Released 1999

Directed by David Koepp

Starring Kevin Bacon

Tom Witzky (Kevin Bacon) doesn't believe in the supernatural, yet after he's hypnotized at a friend's party, he begins to hear and see things no one else can. Witzky soon realizes these fragmented and disturbing encounters are pieces of a puzzle he must solve... at any expense.

The eggs on this DVD aren't too hard to find but they're undocumented interview clips that are quite revealing!

From the main menu of this DVD, scroll down and press Enter over the section "Cast & Crew." Once inside, select the first entry, "Kevin Bacon," and then choose the words "Working with Kevin Bacon." A video will appear featuring actress Katherine Erbe (who plays Bacon's wife, Maggie Witzky) and director David Koepp talking about what it's like to work with Bacon on this film.

Now try the same thing with the "David Koepp" bio—select the entry "Working with David Koepp" to hear Bacon, Erbe, and actress Illeana Douglas (who plays Lisa in the film) chatting about the director.

Strictly Ballroom

Miramax

Released 1992

Directed by Baz Luhrmann

Starring Paul Mercurio, Tara Morice, Bill Hunter, Pat Thomson, Gia Carides, Peter Whitford, Barry Otto

This romantic comedy is about an Australian championship ballroom dancer who is encouraged to dance his own steps by an ugly-duckling dancer, who also wants to be his partner.

This tenth anniversary DVD features audio commentary, a 3D gallery, French and Spanish subtitles, and as a special treat, a featurette entitled "Samba To Slow Fox," an entertaining documentary that inspired *Strictly Ballroom.*

There's also a hidden egg on this DVD.

Insert the disc, and from the main menu, scroll up once and select "Sneak Peeks." Once inside this "Miramax Movies to Remember" page, press the Up Arrow, and a white sparkle will magically appear to the right of the words "Sneak Peeks." Now press Enter to bring up a never-before-released two-minute deleted scene with Wayne (Pip Mushin), Scott (Paul Mercurio), and Fran (Tara Morice) in and outside a market.

Swordfish

Warner Bros.

Released 2001

Directed by Dominic Sena

Starring John Travolta, Hugh Jackman, Halle Berry, Don Cheadle

In this high-tech thriller, John Travolta plays a charismatic mastermind who offers $10 million to an ex-con computer hacker (Hugh Jackman) if he can break into an electronic government slush fund codenamed "Swordfish."

This DVD contains Easter eggs that *can* be accessed from a TV-based DVD player, but it may be easier to find them via a DVD-ROM drive.

Whatever your choice, start the movie and then choose Title 10. This will immediately launch an entertaining Paul Oakenfield music video for "Planet Rock (Swordfish Mix)" strewn with video clips from the film.

Next, try Titles 11 through 18 to access various hidden interview snippets with the cast and crew. (You'll know you've found the eggs when the screen flashes "Password Accepted.")

Title 19 will show a slideshow of preproduction color sketches from *Swordfish*.

The Terminator: Special Edition

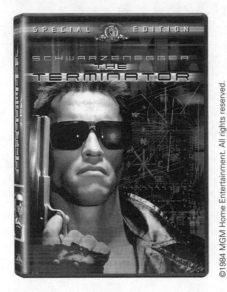

MGM

Released 1984

Directed by James Cameron

Starring Arnold Schwarzenegger, Michael Biehn, Linda Hamilton

In the near future, computers dominate the planet and are bent on exterminating the human race once and for all. To ensure their success, the machines send a seemingly indestructible cyborg (Arnold Schwarzenegger) back in time to kill Sarah Connor (Linda Hamilton), whose unborn son could become mankind's only hope.

Fans of James Cameron's big-budget flick will undoubtedly get a kick out of the many hidden eggs on this rerelease of the film.

Pop in the side of the disc that says "Widescreen," and from the main menu, enter the section entitled "Special Features." Once inside, press the Down Arrow on the remote three times. A small square at the top of the screen will turn green. Press Enter to watch four randomly generated featurettes on the making of the movie.

Another well-hidden collection of five featurettes can be uncovered in the "Languages" section of the DVD. Scroll down to highlight "Français" (under the "Spoken Languages" menu), but instead of pressing Enter, press the Right Arrow, and a box will turn green on the right side of the screen. Press Enter for one of five randomly generated featurettes.

And there's more: Enter the "Scene Selections" area from the main menu, and select "Chapters 13–16," but don't press Enter. Now press the Down Arrow twice to highlight another box at the top of the screen. Press Enter to watch a randomly generated interview segment. There are five.

While still here in the "Scene Selections" area, also try the same thing in "Chapters 25–28" and "Chapters 29–32" for more hidden goodies.

Did You Know?

Lance Henriksen (*Aliens, The Right Stuff, Millennium* TV series) was originally cast as the Terminator, and Arnold Schwarzenegger as the good guy but when "Arnold" read the script, he asked to play the big T.

Apparently, the infamous O.J. Simpson was considered for the role of the Terminator, but the producers were concerned the ex-football star wouldn't be taken seriously.

Terminator 2: Judgment Day (T2: The Ultimate Edition DVD)

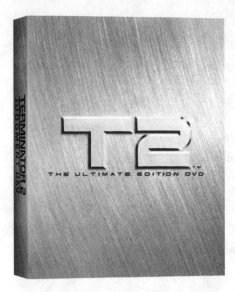

Artisan

Released 1991

Directed by James Cameron

Starring Arnold Schwarzenegger, Linda Hamilton, Edward Furlong, Robert Patrick

Schwarzenegger promised he'd be back, and here he is reprising his role as a T-800 "Terminator." But this time he's been sent back to protect young John Connor (Edward Furlong) and his mother, Sarah (Linda Hamilton), instead of killing them. But a more advanced cyborg (played by Robert Patrick) with shape-shifting abilities also heads back in time to kill Connor before he can grow up to lead the resistance against machines.

Along with the original theatrical version of *Terminator 2: Judgment Day* and the "Special Edition" DVD version, there is a third, undocumented version of the film—planted as an Easter egg.

Pop in the disc with the movie side up (it says "Side A" on the inner rim), and from the main menu, scroll down to select "Special Edition." This will open up another few menu options, and you'll notice there are five odd-looking roman numerals along the right side of the screen.

Here's what to do:

Using your DVD remote, type "8," "2," "9," "9," and "7," which happens to be the date of "judgment day" as prophesized in the film (August 29, 1997). The five symbols along the right side of the screen will spell "The Future Is Not Set" in yellow.

Now press Enter to watch the "Extended Special Edition" of the feature film with extra scenes and an alternate ending. This exciting version is 156 minutes long, and needless to say, a real treat for fans of this sci-fi series.

If accessing this hidden movie is too tough for you, simply start watching any of the two versions, and access Title 3 using your DVD remote to launch this third version.

There are more goodies buried on this DVD. Take out the disc and flip it over to play "Side B" with all the special features on it. At the main menu, do not select from any of these three options; after a half-minute or so, one of three random events will happen:

- The face of a T-1000 will morph out of the center of the screen and tell you to "Get Out!"
- A TV screen will appear and flicker on the bottom-left corner of the screen with the words "Join the Resistance." If you click on it fast enough, it'll take you to a hidden screen written by Connor, telling you about a secret place to go online to train for the upcoming war.
- The same TV screen will show snow again (but without the words "Join the Resistance"). Press Enter and the face of Beethoven will be seen in space, breaking open to reveal the Terminator's face. This is a short "Swelltone" trailer.

The Thing: Collector's Edition

Universal Studios

Released 1982

Directed by John Carpenter

Starring Kurt Russell

©1982 Universal City Studios, Inc.

A deadly alien is awakened from a 100,000-year deep freeze under the Earth's crust and is not too happy about it. An American research team working in the Antarctic tundra is determined to put an end to its wrath, but discovers the creature's ability to morph into other living beings, making it difficult to tell who is human and who is not.

Universal Studios has placed an unannounced feature on this creepy DVD.

From the main menu, select "Bonus Materials" and then choose the "Terror Takes Shape" documentary. From the three options ("Chapter List," "Language Selection," and "Play"), choose "Language Selection," and you will find the entry "Music Score." Once this is selected (by pressing Enter over it), choose the words "Play Movie" to watch the entire documentary—but with just the musical score!

Three Kings

Warner Bros.

Released 1999

Directed by David O. Russell

Starring George Clooney, Mark Wahlberg, Ice Cube, Spike Jonze

This dark comedy takes place during the Gulf War, when four American soldiers search for stolen Kuwaiti gold in the Iraqi desert and are followed by a nosy reporter looking for a story. In the end, the team finds something much more valuable.

From the disc's main menu, select "Special Features" and then choose "Production Notes" near the bottom of the screen. Now select the first entry, "Origins." Once inside, press the Up Arrow on the remote, and a red grenade will appear. Press Enter to watch an entertaining TV spot for *Three Kings*.

Next, go back to the main menu, and select "Special Features" and then the first option, "Cast & Crew." Press the Up Arrow, and another red grenade will appear. Press Enter and take note of this secret code: "SCUD." This is to be used on the *Three Kings* Events web site, accessible through the DVD-ROM portion of the disc. A treasure awaits you if you succeed!

The second password can be found once again in the "Special Features" section of the DVD, but choose the word "Continue" to go to the second, and then third page of features. Now press the Down Arrow on the remote until another red grenade appears. This web site password is "BAGHDAD."

The Tigger Movie

Walt Disney Pictures

Released 2000

Directed by Jun Falkenstein

Starring John Hurt, Jim Cummings, Nikita Hopkins, Ken Sansom, John Fiedler, Peter Cullen, Andre Stojka, Kath Soucie, Tom Attenborough

In this animated tale of friendship, love, and family, a scheme by Tigger's friends—including Winnie the Pooh, Roo, Piglet, Eeyore, Rabbit, and Owl—backfires as they try to cure Tigger's loneliness.

From the main menu, enter the "Bonus Materials" section, and the first entry will be a "Tigger Movie Trivia Game." Select it and if you answer all of the questions correctly, it'll unlock a secret "video prize" discussing the history of Winnie the Pooh including the stuffed animals that inspired the characters, how Walt Disney heard about them, and much more.

If you're having difficulty answering all the multiple-choice questions, select Title 5 on your DVD remote (or by using DVD-ROM software on a computer).

Lora Croft in Tomb Raider

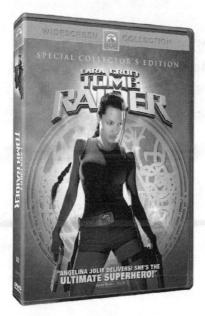

Paramount Pictures

Released 2001

Directed by Simon West

Starring Angelina Jolie

This video game–turned movie casts the sexy Angelina Jolie as British adventurer Lara Croft, resolute to save the world by stopping a time-controlling talisman and ancient key from falling into the wrong hands.

And what sci-fi action flick would be complete without an Easter egg planted on its DVD?

Fom the main menu, go to the "Special Features" section, and press the Down Arrow on the remote two times. The two waves at the bottom of the screen will stop flashing (below the words "Main Menu").

Press Enter for an emotional two-minute interview clip with Jolie and her real-life dad, Jon Voigt, talking about working together on this film.

Did You Know?

Tomb Raider is one of the most popular computer and console video game series of all time. Since its debut in 1996 (on the Sony PlayStation, Sega Saturn, and PC), the game series has sold more than 28 million units worldwide.

Total Recall: Special Limited Edition

Artisan Entertainment

Released 1990

Directed by Paul Verhoeven

Starring Arnold Schwarzenegger

"They stole his mind, now he wants it back" was the tagline for this sci-fi thriller with incredible special effects. In the near future, construction worker Douglas Quaid (Arnold Schwarzenegger) takes a "virtual vacation" on the planet Mars, but when he awakens, finds his friends and family are trying to kill him. Quaid takes a real trip to Mars to unravel an "out of this world" conspiracy.

This cool-looking limited edition DVD—packaged in a round tin designed to look like Mars—features a small Easter egg…if you know where to look.

From the disc's main menu, select the "Setup" tab (second from the bottom). Press Enter to be taken to another menu screen, and scroll down to highlight the words "Main Menu" at the bottom of the screen. Now press the Left Arrow on the remote twice, and the red JVC logo in the corner of the screen will turn white.

Press Enter to view a commercial for JVC products.

Toy Story: The Ultimate Toy Box

Disney Pictures

Released 1995 and 1999

Directed by John Lasseter (*Toy Story*); John Lasseter, Ash Brannon, Lee Unkrich (*Toy Story 2*)

Starring Tom Hanks, Tim Allen, Joan Cusack, Kelsey Grammer, Don Rickles, Jim Varney, Wallace Shawn, John Ratzenberger, Annie Potts

Disney/Pixar's computer-animated feature films are a peek into the (mis)adventures of a child's toys, including the antics of a popular spaceman toy named Buzz Lightyear (Tim Allen) and a cowboy, Sheriff Woody (Tom Hanks).

This "Ultimate Toy Box" box set offers hours of bonus features—but there are also some hidden goodies worth finding, too.

Insert disc 3 and choose "Toy Story 2." Then select "Jesse's Song" in the "Story" section and press the Left Arrow. A question mark will appear on the screen—press Enter to watch a funny outtake (with an explanation) by two of the film's directors, Ash Brannon and John Lasseter.

Also on the same disc, select "Toy Story 2," and then enter the "History" area. Now click on "The Continuing World of Toy Story. " After this short video clip ends (or once you skip to the next frame), there's a hidden menu entitled "Links." Press Enter. This bonus screen houses many other new features to kick back and watch, such as abandoned reels from Woody's Nightmare and Buzz Lightyear's cartoon.

> **Did You Know?**
>
> Toy Story (1995) was the first full-length, computer-animated movie.

Tron: Collector's Edition

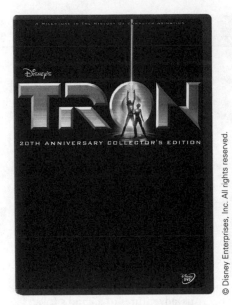

Disney Pictures

Released 1982

Directed by Steven Lisberger

Starring Jeff Bridges, Bruce Boxleitner, David Warner, Cindy Morgan, Barnard Hughes

In this groundbreaking special effects extravaganza, Kevin Flynn (Jeff Bridges) is a hacker who breaks into an ex-employer's computer system to prove they stole his programs, when he finds himself beamed inside of the mainframe. Flynn must fight for his life in a number of gladiator games and find a way to get back to reality.

Insert the second disc and stay on the animated main menu without touching any of the buttons on your DVD remote. Eventually "www. tronkillerapp.com" appears on the screen. If you type that web address into your Internet browser, it'll take you to a secret site.

Also on this second DVD, select "Publicity" on the bottom right of the main menu. Once inside, scroll down to highlight the words "Publicity and Merchandising," but don't press Enter just yet. Instead, press the Down Arrow one more time, and the red words "DVD Credits" will appear on the left of the screen. Press Enter to read who's responsible for this two-disc DVD set.

The Twilight Zone— Vol. 28 to 43

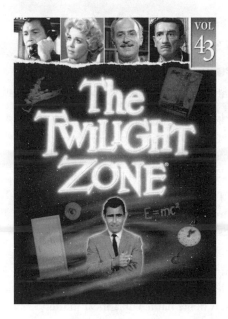

Image Entertainment

TV series 1959–1964

Created by Rod Serling

C reated by visionary writer Rod Serling, the original *Twilight Zone* TV series on CBS (156 episodes in total) proved to be one of the most influential science fiction shows in television history. Tales about aliens, robots, monsters, and magic, were cleverly disguised social commentaries about human life in the 20th century.

View any of the *Twilight Zone* DVDs from Image Entertainment (Volumes 28 through 43), and you can unlock an Easter egg within.

From the main menu, click the Right button on the DVD remote once to highlight "Inside the Twilight Zone." Press Enter and then choose the last entry, "Reviews and Credits."

Now you should see a listing of the four episodes on the DVD. On at least two of them, you can select the episode and press the Right Arrow, which will launch a gray star. Press Enter to be taken to the musical score from that particular episode.

Back in the "Reviews and Credits" page, this time press the Right Arrow twice over your favorite episode, and press Enter to view original product placements and program bumpers from that episode.

Twin Peaks—Season One Box Set

Artisan

TV Series

Began 1990 – 1991 (Two seasons)

Starring Kyle MacLachlan

From the minds of Mark Frost and David Lynch came *Twin Peaks,* a wildly imaginative and critically acclaimed TV drama from the early '90s.

The first season box set features a number of extras—including two Easter eggs on each of the four DVDs.

Pop in any of the discs, and from the main menu, select any episode by scrolling right or left and press Enter. Once inside this new screen, select "Episode Features" and then press the Up Arrow. A beige flame will appear in the upper-left corner of the screen. Press Enter to view secret interview clips.

Here's the breakdown of what you'll find, by episode:

- Disc 1, Episode 1: An interview snippet with director Duwayne Dunham
- Disc 1, Episode 2: An interview snippet with series director of photography Frank Byers
- Disc 2, Episode 3: An interview snippet with director Tina Rathborne (with her son and guinea pig!)
- Disc 2, Episode 4: An interview snippet with director Tim Hunter
- Disc 3, Episode 5: An interview snippet with director Lesli Linka Glatter
- Disc 3, Episode 6: An interview snippet with director Caleb Deschanel
- Disc 4, Episode 7: An interview snippet with series production designer Richard Hoover
- Disc 4, "Tibet" Section: A hidden DVD-credits screen with 14 pages of text and pictures

Also, while on the DVD Credits page that begins "Special Thanks from Three-Legged Cat," press the Up Arrow and a flame will appear on the right. Press Enter to view a scary (and silly) video entitled "Spencer's Rock," featuring actor Michael Anderson from the *Twin Peaks* series.

U.S. Marshals: Special Edition

Warner Bros.

Released 1998

Directed by Stuart Baird

Starring Tommy Lee Jones, Wesley Snipes, Robert Downey Jr.

Oscar-winning Tommy Lee Jones returns as Chief Deputy Samuel Gerard (from 1993's *The Fugitive*), a U.S. Marshal determined to capture Mark Sheridan (Wesley Snipes), an accused murderer, who escapes a devastating plane crash en route to prison. In his manhunt, Gerard is joined by other agents, including John Royce (Robert Downey Jr.).

Trailer fanatics should enjoy the two hidden ones planted on this "Special Edition" DVD.

Insert the side of the disc labeled "Special Features," and from the main menu, scroll down, press Enter over the words "Special Features," and then choose "Fugitive Files."

Now select "History of the U.S. Marshals"—at the end of this featurette will be two secret movie trailers: one for 1994's *Wyatt Earp* and the other for 1973's *Cahill U.S. Marshal.*

Unbreakable

Touchstone Pictures/Buena Vista Pictures

Released 2000

Directed by M. Night Shyamalan

Starring Bruce Willis, Samuel L. Jackson

In this suspenseful supernatural thriller, David Dunn (Bruce Willis) awakens from a deadly train crash as the sole survivor and meets a mysterious stranger, Elijah Price (Samuel L. Jackson), who believes comic-book heroes walk the Earth.

This little-known DVD feature will work on either disc in the double-DVD "Vista Series" package.

From the main menu, watch as pieces of key dialogue from the film scroll from right to left. On disc 1, it'll be lines from Dunn's character (Willis), and disc 2 is of Price (Jackson).

But if you don't touch any of the buttons on the DVD remote, you'll begin to hear the dialogue spoken by the characters instead of just seeing the text fly by.

Did You Know?

In the movie, the character Elijah Price (played by Samuel L. Jackson) says he's called "Mr. Glass" for his brittle physical condition. There are many ways the filmmaker visually reinforces this:

- Price's cane is made of glass.
- He's seen in many reflections such as in mirrors, a TV screen, and a glass picture frame in his art gallery.
- He leaves his card on David Dunn's windshield.

The Usual Suspects: Special Edition

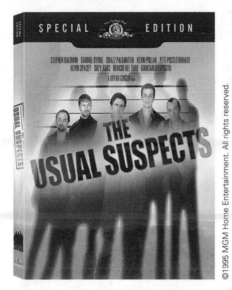

MGM

Released 1995

Directed by Bryan Singer

Starring Gabriel Byrne, Kevin Spacey, Stephen Baldwin, Chazz Palminteri, Pete Postlethwaite, Kevin Pollak

In this award-winning film, five small-time crooks are rounded up as suspects.

"You think you can catch Keyser Soze?"

This "Special Edition" DVD is loaded with features including four featurettes, a gag reel of bloopers, deleted scenes, audio commentary, and more.

To access the Easter eggs, pop the disc in the player with the "Special Features" side facing up. From the animated main menu, press the Up Arrow, and the words "The Usual Suspects" will illuminate in yellow. Press Enter.

This will now take you to a secret menu screen on the DVD with a handful of items that can be selected by pressing the four arrow keys. If you choose the correct items in the proper order, you will unlock two additional featurettes on the DVD—one is an interview with John Ottman, the person responsible for the music in the film, (along with a film historian), and the other is some interview outtakes.

The correct sequence is "Quartet," "Guatemala," then the lady, and finally, the broken cup.

Vanilla Sky

Paramount Pictures

Released 2001

Directed by Cameron Crowe

Starring Tom Cruise, Penélope Cruz, Kurt Russell, Jason Lee, Noah Taylor, Cameron Diaz

David Aames (Tom Cruise) has it all—fame, fortune, youth, good looks, and a woman he loves (Penélope Cruz)—but it all comes crumbling down in a fateful encounter with a jealous lover (Cameron Diaz). The viewer is taken on a rollercoaster ride, continually guessing what's real and what's not.

From the main menu of this DVD, head over to the "Special Features" section and then choose "Photo Galleries." Once inside, scroll up to the words "Special Features," but don't press Enter. Instead, tap the Right Arrow on the DVD remote, and the white mask on the right side of the screen will turn pink.

Now press Enter to view over five minutes of deleted scenes, outtakes, and bloopers.

Did You Know?

Penélope Cruz also starred as Sofia Serrano in the original Spanish version of "Vanilla Sky," entitled "Abre los ojos" ("Open Your Eyes"), directed by Alejandro Amenábar in 1997.

The Wizard of Oz

Warner Bros.

Released 1939

Directed by Victor Fleming

Starring Judy Garland, Ray Bolger, Jack Haley, Bert Lahr

Heralded as the best family film of all time by the American Film Institute, *The Wizard of Oz* tells the tale of the young Dorothy Gale (Judy Garland), who is swept away to a magical, song-filled adventure along the yellow brick road.

From the main menu of this feature-packed DVD, access the "Follow The Road To Oz" section to view a host of special features.

Select "Characters of Oz," and then scroll down and choose Glinda. Press the Up Arrow on the remote, and the yellow globe above her wand will illuminate in yellow. Press Enter to read some undocumented info on the Munchkins. Did you know these hardworking little people spent seven weeks filming at MGM and were paid from $35 to $75 a week (plus room and board)?

Also, on the "Wicked Witch of the West" character screen, press the Up Arrow and a yellow hourglass will appear. Press Enter to read secret facts about the Winged Monkeys.

In fact, if you tap the Left Arrow on many of these character pages, the ruby red slippers in the lower-left of the screen will illuminate, taking you to new hidden pages with additional information about the actors.

X-MEN

20th Century Fox

Released 2000

Directed by Bryan Singer

Starring Patrick Stewart, Ian McKellen

In this popular comic book–turned Hollywood blockbuster, Professor Xavier (Patrick Stewart) helps a group of mutants come to grips with and harness their special powers. Together, they must foil the plot of the sinister Magneto (Ian McKellen), who believes humans and mutants cannot coexist.

The DVD for this sci-fi action flick features two Easter eggs.

The first can be accessed by going to the "Special Features" section; then choose "Theatrical Trailers and TV Spots." Once here, press the Left Arrow, and a yellow rose will appear on the screen. Press Enter and sit back and enjoy a very funny joke played on the cast of the film involving an unexpected visitor.

The second surprise is in the "Art Gallery" area of the "Special Features" section. Press the Right Arrow twice, and Wolverine's dog tags will illuminate. Press Enter to read about two characters—"The Blob" and "The Beast"—who were cut from the film but should appear in the sequel, *X2*. Press the Right Arrow to scroll through six pages of preliminary sketches and drawings.

Zoolander

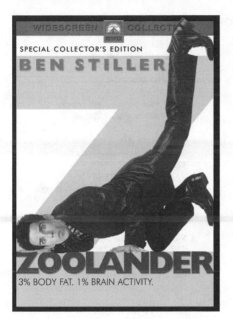

Paramount Pictures

Released 2001

Directed by Ben Stiller

Starring Ben Stiller, Owen Wilson

High fashion meets hilarious comedy in this story about a clueless model, Derek Zoolander (Ben Stiller), who is brainwashed into killing the Prime Minister of Malaysia.

Zoolander contains a little-known—and quite humorous—video clip with commentary.

From the disc's main menu, click on the "Special Features" menu, and then select "More" to get to the second page. Now click on "Photo Galleries," and press the Right Arrow to highlight the spinning *M* symbol on the screen.

Press Enter to watch a rehearsal tape featuring Zoolander (Stiller) and Hansel (Owen Wilson) practicing their climactic "walk-off" catwalk sequence.

Did You Know?

Ben Stiller, who starred, co-wrote, directed, and produced this film, also had his dad, Jerry Stiller, play the role of the slimy "Maury Ballstein." A veteran actor and comedian, Jerry Stiller is best known with today's generation as Frank Costanza from *Seinfeld* (1993-1998), George's neurotic father. His first TV series, however, was 1948's *Toast of the Town*.

INTERNATIONAL CONTACT INFORMATION

AUSTRALIA
McGraw-Hill Book Company Australia Pty. Ltd.
TEL +61-2-9415-9899
FAX +61-2-9415-5687
http://www.mcgraw-hill.com.au
books-it_sydney@mcgraw-hill.com

CANADA
McGraw-Hill Ryerson Ltd.
TEL +905-430-5000
FAX +905-430-5020
http://www.mcgrawhill.ca

GREECE, MIDDLE EAST,
NORTHERN AFRICA
McGraw-Hill Hellas
TEL +30-1-656-0990-3-4
FAX +30-1-654-5525

MEXICO (Also serving Latin America)
McGraw-Hill Interamericana Editores S.A. de C.V.
TEL +525-117-1583
FAX +525-117-1589
http://www.mcgraw-hill.com.mx
fernando_castellanos@mcgraw-hill.com

SINGAPORE (Serving Asia)
McGraw-Hill Book Company
TEL +65-863-1580
FAX +65-862-3354
http://www.mcgraw-hill.com.sg
mghasia@mcgraw-hill.com

SOUTH AFRICA
McGraw-Hill South Africa
TEL +27-11-622-7512
FAX +27-11-622-9045
robyn_swanepoel@mcgraw-hill.com

UNITED KINGDOM & EUROPE
(Excluding Southern Europe)
McGraw-Hill Education Europe
TEL +44-1-628-502500
FAX +44-1-628-770224
http://www.mcgraw-hill.co.uk
computing_neurope@mcgraw-hill.com

ALL OTHER INQUIRIES Contact:
Osborne/McGraw-Hill
TEL +1-510-549-6600
FAX +1-510-883-7600
http://www.osborne.com
omg_international@mcgraw-hill.com